D'AUBIGNÉ'S
MEDITATIONS
SUR LES PSEAUMES

ALAN D. SAVAGE

ARDENS ET VIVENS

PRINCETON THEOLOGICAL SEMINARY

STUDIES IN REFORMED THEOLOGY AND HISTORY is published by Princeton Theological Seminary. All correspondence should be addressed to STUDIES IN REFORMED THEOLOGY AND HISTORY, P.O. Box 821, Princeton, NJ 08542-0803 USA. Fax (609) 497-7829.

MANUSCRIPT SUBMISSIONS

Contributions to STUDIES IN REFORMED THEOLOGY AND HISTORY are invited. Copies of printed and electronic manuscript requirements are available upon request from the Editor at the above address.

COPYRIGHT AND PERMISSIONS

Contents

Editor's Foreword

How widely influential a given text will be is not known at the time of its composition and earliest circulation, especially when it comes to writings produced during such cultural upheavals as the Reformation and Renaissance. Decrees of church councils, formulas of concord, terms of military alliances and treaties, contagious tunes set to poetic paraphrase of Psalms, and so on, have different weight in this or that context and for this or that season. It happens that what was once a most significant document needs to be lifted up again for subsequent generations to have a more accurate appraisal of the forces to which men and women of this period responded and that they helped shape.

Such is the case with Agrippa d'Aubigne's *Meditations* on the Psalms, both because of the extraordinary importance given to the Psalms in individual spirituality and public worship, and because of the precision and power of the language guiding the readers' meditation on the canonical songs. *Poiesis* arises from deep-down knowing; there is a kinesthetic memory set in motion and reinforced by angular truth worthily expressed. The Genevan Psalter had, and has, that dynamic. So to a lesser, but still great, extent, did d'Aubigne's *Meditations*, which nourished and encouraged countless believers caught up in the turbulence of their times.

We leave intact d'Aubigne's own French because the approach that Professor Savage takes, that of sustained literary analysis, would be considerably weakened by the loss of the cadences and vivid language inherent in the energy and nuance of the *Meditations*. There is a beauty, sinewy strength, firm compassion, clarity of thought to the *Meditations* that we have decided belong to its appreciatively recovered prominence.

Alan Savage is a member of the French Department, Wheaton College, Wheaton, Illinois.

—David Willis

Introduction

While traveling through Amboise on their way to Paris in 1560, Jean d'Aubigné and his eight-year-old son Agrippa came upon the horrible spectacle of the decapitated conspirators of Amboise. The father made his son swear to be a defender of the Protestant Cause for which those conspirators had died, and Agrippa did indeed spend his life serving that cause. d'Aubigné's formative years were given over to humanist studies—already at age six "il lisoit aux quatre langues"—first at the hands of private tutors Jean Cottin and Mathieu Béroald, then at the Protestant Academy in Geneva, where he studied under Théodore de Bèze. In 1563, d'Aubigné momentarily abandoned his studies to fight with the Protestant soldiers defending the besieged city of Orléans. In 1568, his studies finished, he took up arms once again, and continued to fight for the best part of the next twenty-five years, during which he played an important role in many major events of the Religious Wars. He became a close friend of Henri de Navarre—the future Henri IV—in whom so many Protestant hopes rested, and was a horrified witness to Henri's wavering back and forth between Protestantism and Catholicism. He tried until the very end to prevent Henri's final abjuration in 1593. For d'Aubigné, Henri's conversion and later his Edict of Nantes both represented unacceptable compromise, so he became a leading voice in Protestant assemblies against such compromise and was active in opposition to the King. He participated in Condé's uprising in 1615 and in the revolt against Luynes in 1620. As a result, his pension was revoked, and he was forced to take up exile in Geneva. In the "Protestant Rome" d'Aubigné carried on with the same enthusiasm and conviction as in France, serving as a member of the city's "conseil de guerre" and also offering his services as a military adviser to other Protestant cities such as Bern, where he helped plan the city's fortification. He remained active until his death in 1630, having witnessed in 1628 the final defeat of the Protestant Cause with the capitulation of La Rochelle to Richelieu's troops.

In addition to being an active soldier, d'Aubigné was a prolific writer. In the latter years of his life, his literary production became as important to his defense of Protestantism as his military exploits had been earlier. With the exception of his first collection of poems, *Printemps*, which he later rejected because it dealt with profane rather than divine love, d'Aubigné's works all revolve around his faith and the "Parti protestant." *Les Tragiques*, first published in 1616, but written for the most part in 1577, gives a poetic account of the Religious Wars. The poet depicts the horrors of the conflicts that ravaged France—with biting satire reserved for those considered responsible, mainly the King, the Princes, and the Roman Catholic Church—in a way that highlights God's control over history and emphasizes the eventual, sure triumph of the true (Protestant) Church. The *Histoire Universelle*, the first volume of which was published in 1618, covers the period from 1550–1602. A counterpart to the *Tragiques*, it gives an "impartial" blow-by-blow account of the events poetically depicted in the epic poem. *Sa vie à ses enfants* is a more personal complement to the *Histoire*, for in it d'Aubigné promises to reveal everything concerning his own life, including things that were not appropriate for the *Histoire*. *Du debvoir mutuel* and the *Traitté des guerres civiles* of 1621 address political questions concerning matters of religion and freedom of conscience, questions so important during the religious conflicts in France and elsewhere. *Les Aventures du Baron Faeneste* of 1617 (vol. 1–2), 1619 (vol. 3), and 1630 (vol. 4), and *La Confession catholique du sieur de Sancy*, which was not published until 1660, continue and amplify the satirical treatment of the men of power found in the *Tragiques*. Finally, the *Petites oeuvres meslees*, published in 1630, contain religious verse—*Hiver* and *La Création*—along with psalm paraphrases and the *Meditations sur les Pseaumes*.

For an author of such an extensive body of work, d'Aubigné has received remarkably little attention throughout the years, although fortunately the past three decades have brought about somewhat of a renaissance in d'Aubigné studies. Once thought to be of only limited literary talent, he is now recognized by many as one of the major literary figures of the sixteenth century. In their studies of d'Aubigné, critics have turned first and foremost to *Les Tragiques*, and have found it to be a carefully crafted, profoundly original work that provides deep insight into the social, political, and religious context of the times. Regrettably, this attention given the *Tragiques* has been, in many ways, to the exclusion of d'Aubigné's other works, which are often considered secondary at best or even summarily dismissed.

A few recent critics have, however, turned their attention to the rest of d'Aubigné's writings, and in doing so have demonstrated the richness of these works, including the *Meditations sur les Pseaumes*. Most notably, Marie-Madeleine Fragonard in her *La Pensée religieuse d'Agrippa d'Aubigné et son expression* and Catherine Randall Coats in her *Subverting the System: d'Aubigné and Calvinism*, building on Michel Jeanneret's seminal study of the meditations in his *Poésie et tradition biblique au XVIe siècle*, have shown how the *Meditations* fit into d'Aubigné's thematic and stylistic universe. These studies represent the most in-depth work on d'Aubigné's *Meditations* done to date. In both cases, the work is considered essentially in its relationship to d'Aubigné's overall literary enterprise. No single study devoted entirely to the *Meditations* exists, and it is therefore the object of the present study to provide such an analysis. The *Meditations* merit such attention. First, because meditation played an essential role in both Protestant and Catholic spirituality in the sixteenth century, the *Meditations sur les Pseaumes* are an important text for understanding the particular development and nature of this devotional practice and its literary manifestations among Huguenots. Moreover, because meditation is an exercise that consists in appropriating a set of beliefs and constructing an identity based on those beliefs, the *Meditations* are also essential for understanding the development of the Huguenot "self." They forge a very specific identity in the way they address various theological, social, political, and literary questions.

Unlike the *Tragiques*, which stands in a class of its own, d'Aubigné's *Meditations* are actually one of a small, relatively homogeneous group of prose psalm meditations written (mainly by Protestant authors, but not exclusively so) in the latter half of the sixteenth century and the early years of the seventeenth century. The genre of psalm meditation that developed in the sixteenth century was an outgrowth of the renewed interest in the psalms brought about by the religious reforms of the times. Early in the century, the psalms became the object of translations and paraphrases in the vernacular, from which the meditations were a natural development. Both Protestants and Catholics participated in these literary and spiritual exercises, but from early on the psalms played an especially important role in the lives of the Protestants, mainly as a result of Calvin's successful efforts in using the psalms as an integral part of Huguenot devotional life, both individual and communal. Capitalizing on the spiritual significance of the psalms in order to meet a definite need in the Protestant public, Théodore de Bèze offered his *Chrestiennes Méditations* in 1582,

> ayant choisi . . . les sept Psalmes pieça nommez penitentiaux, pour estre
> lors specialement dediez à ceux lesquels après avoir satisfait à la peni-
> tence publique et canonique, estoyent r'alliez au corps de l'Eglise. . . .[1]

The fact that in three years there appeared as many editions of the collection, plus an English translation, speaks to the importance of this type of devotional writing.

Building on the model presented in Bèze's *Chrestiennes Méditations*, several authors (four Protestants and two Catholics) published collections of prose psalm meditations. Because, for the most part, the Protestant authors were more accustomed to the type of interaction with the psalms fostered by this type of writing, their meditations developed more fully the potentialities of the genre. Generally speaking, with the Protestant authors there is an evolution from the very strict adherence to the biblical text and the single theological purpose found in Bèze's work, to a more free stylistic treatment of the psalms that is concerned not only with penitence but also with other aspects of the faith, especially as it relates to contemporary circumstances.

d'Aubigné, of whom Henri Weber says, "ses débats intérieurs, ses repentirs et ses extases offrent . . . comme l'itinénaire exemplaire de la conscience protestante,"[2] occupies an interesting place within this group of Protestant meditation authors. His *Meditations*, the last of the meditation collections to be published, were composed over a long period of time spanning the last Religious Wars and the final establishment of peace: 1588–1626. As a result, his texts can be seen as an embodiment of the salient characteristics of the prose psalm meditations, for, covering such a long time period, they demonstrate the various dynamics of this type of meditation as it developed over the years. d'Aubigné's own life and role in the period are directly related to these dynamics. Because he was one of the "fermes" of the Huguenot Party, intransigent and noncompromising, it is not surprising to see that his meditations are among the most strongly attached to the biblical text. On the other hand, as the poet of the *Tragiques*, d'Aubigné was a master of marshalling poetic *inventio* for the cause, and his meditations are also among the most highly imaged and stylistically rich. Thus, in addition to demonstrating the relationship between this form of writing and its historical—both theological and political—

---

[1] Théodore de Bèze, *Chrestiennes Méditations*, ed. Mario Richter, Collection Textes Littéraires Français (Geneva: Droz, 1964), Introduction.

N.B. The quotes in French in the present book have been taken from some texts that have not been modernized, as is the case for Bèze's *Méditations*, and from others that have, as is the case for Calvin's *Institution*. No attempt has been made on my part to modernize the versions quoted in the original sixteenth-century French.

[2] Weber, notes on d'Aubigné's *Meditations*, in *Oeuvres* (Paris: Gallimard, 1969), p. 1252.

context, d'Aubigné's *Meditations sur les Pseaumes* display in sharp relief the tension between fidelity to the biblical text and personal invention inherent to the genre.

Furthermore, d'Aubigné's *Meditations* present the richest paratext,[3] and the various paratextual elements of the work—notably the preface and the *Occasions et Arguments* that introduce each meditation—shed important light on the nature and function of this text in its immediate context. Specifically, in the preface, d'Aubigné focuses on Scripture in terms of language and style, and he offers his meditations "en simplicité du langage de Canaan." The expression provides the basis for analyzing and understanding the *Meditations* as the manifestation of a language; that is, of a social phenomenon that both shapes the way an individual sees the world and is itself shaped by the world in which it is spoken. In other words, in the *Meditations* the "langage de Canaan" (i.e., the Bible as interpreted and appropriated by the Huguenots) gives the believers the spiritual framework within which to interpret and express their world. At the same time, the theological, social, and political context of the meditations, of which the *Occasions et Arguments* speak, firmly ground the spiritual principles of the Kingdom in a specific set of circumstances that in turn affect the way the "langage de Canaan" is "spoken." This dual nature of the "langage de Canaan" is especially evident in the way d'Aubigné "speaks" it in the *Meditations*—that is, the different ways in which he incorporates the text of the Bible into his own text—for the interrelation between Scripture and the narrative context assimilating it reveals the way each affects the other and it is thus the locus for the fashioning of the meditator's identity in relation to the authority of Scripture. In the end one sees that the form and content of the *Meditations* embody the "langage de Canaan" in and through which the Huguenots attempted to express themselves and live out their faith in their sixteenth-century world.

Accordingly, the following study will explore the *Meditations* as a manifestation of the "langage de Canaan" by examining both the context in which the work was written as well as the dynamics of the work itself. Chapter one analyzes the differences between Protestant and Catholic meditative practices, which were a direct result of the very divergent reading practices of each group. Chapter two delves into the meaning of the important phrase "en simplicité du langage de Canaan" that d'Aubigné uses to characterize his prose psalm meditations. The third chapter examines the specific ways that

---

[3] Genette defines paratext as "ce par quoi un texte se fait livre et se propose comme tel à ses lecteurs et plus particulièrement au public" (Gérard Genette, *Seuils* [Paris: Editions du Seuil, 1987], p. 5).

d'Aubigné speaks the "langage de Canaan" in the *Meditations* by appropriating Scripture; that is, by incorporating the biblical text into his own narrative context in the individual meditations. By exploring these three areas, this study shows the important place the *Meditations sur les Pseaumes* held in the Huguenot literature of the late sixteenth century. In the final analysis, the *Meditations* embody, in form and content, the "langage de Canaan" that is intimately linked with Huguenot identity. In this manner, they demonstrate how a specific genre developed in relation to a specific set of beliefs and social practices and constituted a locus for defining, in both its private and public dimensions, the identity related to those beliefs.

I

Prose Psalm Meditations

Any attempt to understand the "langage de Canaan" of the prose psalm meditations must begin by placing this group of works within the context that gave rise to them. First considered are the specifics of Bible-reading practices in the sixteenth century and their relationship to the production of devotional texts. Then, the main literary characteristics of the prose psalm meditations are reviewed. An examination of these two areas will elucidate the genesis and composition of d'Aubigné's *Les Meditations sur les Pseaumes*.

PROTESTANTS AND THE BIBLE

"La cognoissance de Dieu" is one of the fundamental, reoccurring themes of Huguenot literature of the sixteenth century. In the *Epistre au Roi*, the dedicatory epistle to his *L'Institution chrétienne*, John Calvin clearly states the case of the French Protestants, on whose behalf he was writing:

> Considérez, Sire, toutes les parties de notre cause, et nous jugez être les plus pervers des pervers, si vous ne trouvez manifestement que nous sommes oppressés et recevons injures et opprobres, parce que nous mettons notre espérance en Dieu vivant (I Tim. 4:10), parce que nous croyons que c'est la vie éternelle de connaître un seul vrai Dieu, et celui qu'il a envoyé, Jésus-Christ (Jean 17:3).[4]

Calvin then goes on to explain that this knowledge of God should be the intimate, personal experience of every believer, and, not surprisingly, just how

---

[4] Jean Calvin, "Au Roi de France Très Chrétien, François Premier de ce nom, son Prince et souverain seigneur, Jean Calvin, Paix et salut en Notre Seigneur Jésus-Christ," *L'Institution chrétienne* (Paris: Editions Farel, 1978), pp. xxiv–xxv.

1

one can come to know God in this way is one of the major topics of the
Institution. For Calvin, the first signs of a God who can be known are man's
innate sense of a divine being's existence and the testimony of nature, but because these two means of revelation are not enough for man in his natural
state, God provided Scripture in order to make himself known to fallen man.[5]
Calvin's sentiments are echoed in the preface to the Geneva Bible of 1562,
which begins with a different formulation of the same conviction:

> Comme c'est le plus excellent thresor que Dieu puisse eslargir aux hommes,
> que de les amener à la cognoissance de nostre Seigneur Iesus Christ,
> d'autant que tout leur bien & leur salut gist en cela, aussi n'y a il chose
> en quoy l'ingratitude du monde se monstre mieux, qu'en ce qu'un tel
> benefice est si peu prise de ceux à qui il est presenté. Ce qui se voit
> ouvertement en cela, que la parole de Dieu, laquelle est le moyen du-
> quel il se veut servir pour nous faire venir à la cognoissance de son Fils,
> est si mal receuë de la plus grande partie des hommes.[6]

Although the context here is somewhat different—dealing with the neglect of
Scripture—the underlying principle is identical: fallen man can attain saving
knowledge of God through the Bible.

Sola scriptura. Luther's expression indeed sums up Protestants' convictions
concerning the Bible. For them, in the midst of the many uncertainties of
man's existence, the Bible was the one and only sure guide to the true meaning of life and alone led to the true knowledge of God. The "Au Lecteur" of
the Geneva Bible is an eloquent testimony to this conviction:

> C'est la voye certaine pour nous guider. . . . C'est la vraye reigle pour dis-
> cerner entre le bien et le mal. . . . C'est la lumiere qui nous redresse. . . .
> C'est l'escole de toute sagesse. . . . c'est le miroir auquel nous contem-
> plons la face de Dieu. . . . C'est le sceptre royal, par lequel il nous gouv-

---

[5] "Nous mettons hors de doute que les hommes aient un sentiment de divinité en eux, même
d'un mouvement naturel. Car, afin que nul ne cherchât son refuge sous titre d'ignorance, Dieu
a imprimé en tous une connaissance de soi-même, de laquelle il renouvelle tellement la mémoire,
comme s'il en distillait goutte à goutte, afin que quand nous connaissons depuis le premier
jusqu'au dernier qu'il y a un Dieu, et qu'il nous a formés, nous soyons condamnés par notre propre témoignage, de ce que nous ne l'aurons point honoré, et que nous n'aurons point dédié notre
vie à lui obéir" (*Institution*, *Livre I*, p. 9), and "Or parce que la souveraine félicité et le but de
notre vie gît en la connaissance de Dieu, afin que nul n'en fût forclos, non seulement il a gravé
cette semence de religion que nous avons dite en l'esprit des hommes, mais aussi il s'est tellement
manifesté à eux en ce bâtiment tant beau et exquis du ciel et de la terre, et journellement s'y montre et présente, qu'ils ne sauraient ouvrir les yeux qu'ils ne soient contraints de l'apercevoir"
(*Institution*, *Livre I*, p. 17).

[6] "A Tous Vrais Amateurs de la Parole de Dieu, grace & paix par nostre Seigneur Jesus Christ,"
*La Bible qui est toute la saincte escriture, contenant le vieil testament, le nouveau testament; ou, la vieille
& nouvelle alliance* (Geneva: François Iaquy, 1562), p. iiir.

erne comme son peuple. . . . C'est l'instrument de son alliance faite avec nous. . . . C'est le tesmoignage de sa bonne volonté. . . . C'est la pasture unique de nos ames. . . . Bref, c'est le seul moyen en quoy nous differons d'avec les payens & infideles, entant que nous avons une religion asseuree & fondee en la verité infaillible de Dieu. . . .[7]

Of course, such a statement concerning the uniqueness and reliability of Scripture was, in and of itself, really nothing new. It was, however, only part of the Protestants' new found emphasis on the Bible. What follows in the "Au Lecteur" reveals the full implications of the *sola scriptura*:

Aussi sur ce passage i'auroye à taxer la presomption diabolique de ceux qui osent priver le commun peuple de ce benefice de Dieu, luy interdisant la lecture de l'Escriture saincte: comme si Dieu n'avoit point declaré que son intention a esté de la publier à tous estats & à toutes Langues.[8]

The emphasis was thus on the individual believer's contact with the Bible, which, as this somewhat virulent attack shows, constituted a major difference with the Catholic doctrine that considered the Church a necessary mediator between laymen and Scripture. Protestants wanted all people to have a personal contact with the Word of God, and for that reason making the Scriptures accessible was one of the key goals of the Reformers.

The desire for a much closer contact with Scripture for all believers, which manifested itself practically in a call for the proclamation and preaching of the true gospel and for translations in the vernacular, actually originated with Evangelical Humanists like Erasmus and Lefèvre d'Etaples early in the century. In his *Avertissement au Lecteur* of the *Paraphrasis in Evangelium Matthaei*, Erasmus writes:

Pour moi, d'accord avec saint Jérôme, je me féliciterais plutôt de la gloire de la croix, je considérerais le résultat comme particulièrement magnifique et triomphal, si toutes les langues, toutes les races la célébraient, si le laboureur, aux marches de la charrue, chantait en sa langue quelques couplets des psaumes mystiques, si le tisserand, devant son métier, modulait quelque passage de l'Evangile, soulageant ainsi son travail. . . .[9]

Although Erasmus and others like him worked within the framework of the Catholic Church, on the whole this evangelical tendency was not well received

---

[7] "Au Lecteur," *La Bible qui est toute la saincte escriture, contenant le vieil testament, le nouveau testament; ou, la vieille & nouvelle alliance* (Geneva: François Iaquy, 1562), p. iir.

[8] Ibid.

[9] Quoted by Michel Jeanneret, *Poésie et tradition biblique au XVIe siècle* (Paris: José Corti, 1969), p. 20.

by the Church, which eventually came to associate it with schism and heresy.[10] It was, on the other hand, one of the hallmarks of the Protestant faith. Théodore de Bèze's remarks in his "La confession de foi du chrétien" provide a concise summary of the Protestant stand on this issue:

> Comment, ainsi, pourra-t-on être affermi en la sainte et vraie doctrine, consolé dans des tentations si nombreuses et diverses, averti pour résister aux fausses doctrines, sinon en méditant nuit et jour, comme dit David, la Parole de Dieu, et en examinant soigneusement les passages de la sainte Ecriture? . . . nous entendons que chacun doit lire l'Ecriture et en avoir la connaissance. . . . Et quiconque empêche la lecture des Ecritures ôte, en même temps au pauvre peuple le seul moyen de consolation et de salut.[11]

Such declarations did not remain pious wishes; the Reformers worked with great fervor to help believers become intimately acquainted with the Scriptures. This can be seen in the vast program of Bible translation, publication, and diffusion undertaken by the Protestants. The Olivetan Bible, which served as the base text for the Geneva Bible throughout the sixteenth century, was first published in 1535 in Neuchâtel. It was revised in 1536, 1538, 1539, 1540, 1543, 1546, 1551, 1553, 1560, and 1588. From 1550 to 1600, over 290 editions of the Geneva Bible revisions were printed, mainly in Geneva, but also in Lyons and Paris. Compared with the approximately 82 editions of Catholic Bibles in the vernacular printed during the same period (44 of which were editions of the Benoist version, which was not officially accepted by the Church), this number reveals the phenomenal importance of the Bible in Protestant life.[12]

This vast program of Bible diffusion was the central point of the education of believers that the Reformers were seeking to accomplish. For them, the Scriptures had for too long been hidden from the nonclergy, and they thus endeavored with parental-like care to open up the treasures of the Bible for the laity. One of the earliest manifestations of this concern is Farel's *Le Pater Noster et le Credo en françoys*, first published in 1524. In the preface entitled "A tous fideles salut en Jesu Christ," he explains the genesis of the work:

---

[10] S. L. Greenslade, ed., *The Cambridge History of the Bible*, vol. 2: *The West From the Reformation to the Present Day* (Cambridge: Cambridge University Press, 1963), p. 113.

[11] Théodore de Bèze, "La Confession de foi du chrétien," ed. Michel Réveillaud, *La Revue Réformée. Soli Deo Gloria* 6 (1955), p. 64. Calvin makes a similar remark: "nul ne peut avoir seulement un petit goût de saine doctrine pour savoir qui est Dieu, jusqu'à ce qu'il ait été à cette école pour être enseigné par l'Ecriture sainte; car de là procède le commencement de toute droite intelligence, quand nous recevons révéremment tout ce que Dieu y a voulu testifier de soi" (*Institution, Livre I*, p. 34).

[12] See Bettye Thomas Chambers, *Bibliography of French Bibles. Fifteenth- and Sixteenth-Century French Language Editions of the Scriptures* (Geneva: Droz, 1983).

Pourtant affin que chescun puisse prier en sorte qu'il entende ce qu'il dit, en ce petit livret que facilement on pourra porter en la main par tout, est contenue l'orayson dominicale et les articles de la foy contenus au credo, avec familiere exposition de tous deux, affin que plus facilement puissent estre entendus dez simples gens, qui ne sont point exercités en la saincte escriture, et aussy pour avoir quelque acces à ycelle, qui est la table an laquelle tout Chrestien doit prandre sa refection, et sa rigle de vivre.[13]

Similar concerns motivated the editors of the Geneva Bible, who came up with various aids, such as introductions, tables, and notes, to help readers comprehend the sacred text. The editor of the 1562 edition explains:

Ioint aussi que i'ay consideré que les livres qui s'impriment en la langue Françoise, ne sont pas tant pour les gens sçavans & bien exercez en la saincte escriture, comme pour ceux qui n'ont pas cognoissance de la langue Latine, & n'ont pas tel iugement qu'ils n'ayent besoin qu'on leur esclaircisse des points. . . .[14]

The translation of the Bible into the vernacular was thus not enough in itself. It was an essential step, but one that had to be accompanied by a ministry of teaching in order for the "simple gens" to benefit from it. This need for instruction is clearly spelled out in article XXV of the French Confession of Faith of 1559:

Or parce que nous ne jouissons de Jésus-Christ que par l'Evangile, nous croyons que l'ordre de l'Eglise qui a été établi en son autorité doit être sacré et inviolable, et pourtant que l'Eglise ne peut consister, sinon qu'il y ait des pasteurs, qui aient la charge d'enseigner, lesquels on doit honorer et écouter en révérence quand ils sont dûment appelés et exercent fidèlement leur office.[15]

Because Christ is known only through the gospel, the Church can properly function only when this gospel is correctly interpreted and proclaimed by the preacher. Indeed, for Protestants the preacher had a *prophetic* role, a prophet being one who takes the already written Word and brings it alive, as a word from God, for the congregation, revealing its meaning and significance for

---

[13] Guillaume Farel, *Le Pater Noster et le Credo en françoys*, ed. Francis Higman (Geneva: Droz, 1982), pp. 37–38.

[14] "A Tous Vrais Amateurs de la Parole de Dieu . . .," p. iiiv. The title page of this edition of the Bible says: "Aussi avec les figures, on a adjousté des Annotations, fort amples sur toute la Bible."

[15] Olivier Fatio, ed., *Confessions et catéchismes de la foi réformée* (Geneva: Labor et Fides, 1986), p. 123.

them in the present time.[16] Hence, preaching was considered an integral part of church life. In his "La Confession de foi du chrétien," Bèze explains that the reading of the Scriptures must be accompanied by "leur pure prédication et leur exposition: c'est pour cela que les docteurs et les pasteurs sont ordonnés dans l'Eglise."[17] Protestants thus had a twofold approach to the assimilation of the Bible: public exposition and explanation, and private reading and meditation. They considered the two in every way complementary; there was no question of having one without the other.

It is important to point out, however, that, at least during the sixteenth century, the sermon often played a more important role than the actual reading of the Bible. In spite of the mass diffusion of the Scriptures in Protestant circles, few people actually owned a complete Bible (Genevans being a notable exception). In addition, the literacy rate was very low. As a result, instruction had necessarily to be based more on oral transmission than on the assimilation of the printed page. Janine Garrison, in her book *Les Protestants au XVIe siècle*, describes the typical importance of sermons for sixteenth-century Protestants:

> Au XVIe siècle, peu nombreux sont ceux qui possèdent le privilège du savoir-lire. Les autres n'entrent pas directement en contact avec la Bible; il leur faut l'intermédiaire du pasteur, lecteur et interprète des Ecritures. Chaque prêche—et les protestants en ont deux par semaine—s'appuie sur un texte biblique abondamment commenté; l'imprégnation est si profonde qu'en ces mémoires coutumières de la transmission orale le livre saint est inscrit, comme gravé.[18]

This use of the Scriptures inside the "community church" was complemented by its use in the "family church;" Calvin clearly taught the importance of family devotional practices. Indeed, a major part of the religious life and instruction of the Huguenots took place in the home. In his article "L'Education protestante jadis et naguère," Pierre Tirel emphasizes the fact that Protestant

---

[16] For a full treatment of this subject, see Marguerite Soulié, *L'Inspiration biblique dans la poésie religieuse d'Agrippa d'Aubigné* (Paris: Klincksieck, 1977). She explains: "Dès lors qu'est-ce que la prophétie dans l'Eglise, sinon une prédication de la Parole, pourvu que l'on n'oublie pas que toute prédication est vaine si le Saint-Esprit ne l'atteste comme vraie et puissante, plus pénétrante que le glaive à deux tranchants.

Les théologiens et les prédicateurs de Genève avaient bien la même conception de la 'prophétie' puisqu'ils désignaient par ce nom une étude biblique préalable, groupant pasteurs et docteurs, où, après avoir demandé l'illumination au Seigneur, on étudiait sérieusement une page de la Bible, en dégageant son sens actuel, l'engagement concret que le texte allait demander aussi bien au prédicateur qu'aux fidèles, réunis pour entendre la Parole salvatrice qui purifiait les coeurs et consacrait les vies au Seigneur des Seigneurs. Après cette étude placée sous l'invocation du Saint-Esprit, chacun s'en allait prêcher sur le texte ainsi 'réveillé' . . ." (p. 41).

[17] Bèze, *"La Confession,"* p. 64.

[18] Janie Garrison, *Les Protestants au XVIe siècle* (Paris: Fayard, 1988), pp. 35–36.

parents, especially in the early years of the Reformation, felt the pressure to master the Bible not only for their own spiritual life, but also for the religious education of their children.[19] One typical example of family devotional practices is the so-called "veillées paysanes," during which the Scriptures were read and commented upon by either the father, or, if necessary, a more learned male of the community. Such practices, coupled with church life, resulted in an intimate acquaintance with the Scriptures.

On both the theoretical and the practical levels, then, the Bible was the center of each Protestant believer's life as he worked to know God. Although Scripture as a whole was the object of Protestant teaching and reflection, one book held a privileged position: the Book of Psalms. The Reformers, like many before them, believed it to be a sort of summary of the whole Bible. Luther called it a "little Bible." One of the "Arguments" for the Book of Psalms from an English translation of the Geneva Bible explains its contents in the following way:

> This booke of Psalms is set forth unto us by the holy Ghost to be esteemed as a most precious treasure, wherein all things are contayned that appertayne to true felicitie as well in this lyfe present as in the life to come. For the riches of true knowledge and heavenly wisdom are here set open for us, to take thereof most abundantly. . . . Briefly, here we have most present remedies against all temtations, and troubles of minde and conscience, so that being well practised herein, we may be assured against all dangers in this life, lived in the true feare, and love of God, and at length attaine to that incorruptible crowne of glorie, which is layd up for all them that love the coming of our Lord Jesus Christ.[20]

Not surprisingly, it was considered the perfect book for use in instruction and personal devotion, because it set all the essential teachings of the Bible before the believer.

This high regard for the psalms must be understood in context, however, for it was not a uniquely Protestant phenomenon.[21] The importance of the psalms for Calvinists was in many ways the outgrowth of the emphasis that had already been placed on the psalms during the Middle Ages. The Psalter, in Latin, was one of the few books that the medieval Church allowed laymen to possess. It was used as an integral part of devotional practices, especially in the area of penitence. As such, the psalms were among the most widely read

---

[19] Pierre Tirel, "L'Education protestante jadis et naguère," in *La Réforme et l'éducation*, sous la direction de Jean Boisset (Toulouse: Privet, 1974), p. 14.

[20] *Old Testament* (London: Christopher Bakar, 1576), p. 219.

[21] See Jeanneret's *Poésie et tradition biblique*, which contains an in-depth look at the role of the psalms in the sixteenth century. I am greatly indebted to Jeanneret's treatment of the subject.

biblical passages for both the clergy and the laity, and they were often known by heart. Moreover, they were not solely reserved for the sacred practices of the Church but were also used in many profane areas, such as the teaching of Latin grammar. In fact, so widespread and pervasive was the use of the Latin psalms in both the ecclesiastical and secular realms that by the end of the Middle Ages there had been a definite "overkill." David's verses had in many cases become the object of mindless repetition, with the spiritual significance often forgotten or simply misunderstood.

The Book of Psalms was thus a perfect candidate for the humanistic and evangelical reforms of the sixteenth century. The need for a return to the source of a text and its original meaning could not have been better exemplified than by this text, which had in many ways become meaningless. Hence, early in the century the psalms became a subject of concern for the Evangelicals, who hoped to cleanse the biblical text of all additions that it had received over the years (notably the medieval glosses) and to present a faithful translation in a language (French or Latin) accessible to everyone. Erasmus and Lefèvre d'Etaples were among those who turned their attention to the Hebrew poems. Although there were fundamental differences in the way in which each approached the text—Erasmus saw the psalms as the source of practical moral teachings and Lefèvre viewed them as the source of a mystical experience bringing union with God—they both exemplify the Evangelicals' affection for the psalms and their desire to rediscover the Hebrew poems' spiritual significance.

Although the Evangelicals' emphasis on the psalms was strong and consistent, its influence was limited. The translations of the psalms early in the century and the attempts by Evangelicals and humanists to share their enthusiasm for them remained scattered efforts, lacking a sufficiently central goal. These early works did serve, however, as precursors for the undertaking that would crystallize the needed central purpose: the Huguenot Psalter. The man behind the project, John Calvin, had a clear goal he wished to attain: a faithful poetic translation of the psalms, which could be set to music, to be used as the main devotional text for Protestants. His choice of the psalms was based on the fact that he saw in them "comme une anatomie de toutes les affections de l'âme," as well as his own personal interest in the Hebrew poems. Aware that the need for this devotional collection was great and immediate, Calvin put his strong organizational skills to work to bring about the realization of the project.

Calvin also put his own poetic skills to work, translating many of the psalms himself. Yet he soon recognized a superior poet and translator in Clement Marot, who had begun his own psalm translations under the influence of

Marguerite de Navarre. When the *Aulcuns pseaulmes et cantiques mys en chant*[22] was first published in 1539, it contained thirteen translations by Marot and five or more by Calvin. In later editions, Calvin's translations were replaced by new ones by Marot, who eventually took up residence in Geneva after having been exiled from France. In order to understand the originality and high literary quality of Marot's paraphrases, one must recall the medieval practices of psalm translations into French (which, although very rare, did exist). The medieval authors either gave such literal renditions of the Latin, from which they translated, that it was incomprehensible in French, or, at the other extreme, they used so much liberty and added so much to the text that the original became lost. Unlike them, Marot worked from the Hebrew text, giving as literal a translation as possible without making the French awkward or difficult, and attempted to re-create the formal characteristics of Hebrew poetry, such as the laws of parallelism and the independence of the different parts of each poem. Thus, although very conscious of the religious dimension of his work, Marot did not neglect the stylistic dimension, and his translations are among the best of the century. Those who later worked to finish the job he left incomplete, such as Théodore de Bèze, were never able to attain the same fidelity to both the original meaning and the poetic beauty of David's poems.

The diffusion of the Huguenot Psalter, consisting first of Marot's paraphrases, and then later of both Marot's and Bèze's work, was rapid and efficacious. It quickly became an integral part of the French Protestants' lives. The poetic and metrical nature of the psalms strengthened and added to their doctrinal importance, for the early Reformers, especially Calvin, well understood the importance of music in the life of devotion. Calvin writes: "Et à la verité, nous congnoissons par experience, que le chant a grand force & vigueur d'esmouvoir & enflamber le coeur des hommes, pour invoquer et louer Dieu d'un zèle plus vehement et ardent."[23] The translated psalms, which were easily set to music, were considered the most appropriate subject matter for communal singing:

> Nul ne peut chanter chose digne de Dieu, sinon qu'il l'ayt receue d'iceluy: parquoy, quand nous aurons bien circui par tout pour cercher ça et là, nous ne trouverons meuilleures chansons ne plus propres pour ce faire, que les pseaumes de David, lesquels le sainct Esprit lui a dictés et

---

[22] Clément Marot, *Aulcuns pseaulmes et cantiques mys en chant* (Strasbourg, 1539).
[23] Jean Calvin, "Epistre au Lecteur," in Pierre Pidoux, *Le Psautier Huguenot du XVIe siècle. Mélodies et documents. Deuxième volume: Documents et bibliographie* (Bâle: Edition Baerenreiter, 1962), p. 17.

faits. Et pour tant, quand nous les chantons, nous sommes certains que Dieu nous met en la bouche les paroles, comme si luy-même chantoit en nous pour exalter sa gloire.[24]

In this manner, singing the psalms was a form of true worship, allowing God to "exalter sa gloire" through the believers' singing of what God himself had revealed. Protestants saw this as the ultimate step in the knowledge of God, for it represented a complete identification with him and was the expression of his life in them. It is not surprising that the Huguenots found such strength and comfort in the recitation of the Davidic verses, for in doing so, they felt they were performing more than an empty repetition; rather, they were communing with God by allowing him to speak his truth into their daily lives.

The Huguenots' attachment to the psalms was solidified by the many parallels they saw between themselves and the people of Israel, which was one of the common themes of Huguenot literature of the latter half of the sixteenth century.[25] Although this comparison was based on all of the Old Testament (indeed, the whole Bible; the book of Revelation also played a very important role), the Huguenots naturally concentrated on the psalms. A poignant example of this is found in the preface to *L'Exercise de l'ame fidele, assavoir Prieres et Meditations pour se consacrer en toutes sortes d'afflictions* by Daniel Toussain, in which the pastor recalls the first massacre in Orléans on September 5, 1568:

Car des ce jour là qui estoit un Dimanche, moy ayant fait presche de six heures en l'Estape, lequel lieu nous restoit alors, & ayant & trop à propos helâs en ce dernier presche, exposay ce passage du seziesme de sainct Marc, sur l'histoire de la passion: Mon Dieu, Mon Dieu, pourquoy m'as tu laissé! Car jusques la justement estois-je venu en l'exposition de sainct Marc: monsieur de Gallars, lors aussi ministre de ladite Eglise, ayant faict le presche de huict heures au mesme lieu, & suyvant l'ordre des psaumes qu'on chantoit, ayant chanté ce pseaume funebre & lamentable qui venoit à propos, sans toutefois qu'on l'eust choisi, assavoir le pseaume 88. qui est le dernier, qui a esté chanté dans Orleans en l'assemblee de l'Eglise, où entre autres choses, il est dit.

---

[24] Jean Calvin, "A tous Chrestiens et amateurs de la Parole de Dieu, Salut," in Pierre Pidoux, *Le Psautier Huguenot*, p. 21.

[25] This was especially the case during the Religious Wars. As Soulié explains: "les Réformés revêtaient aisément la personnalité d'Isräel. Nul besoin de comparaison, aucun passage entre le passé biblique et le présent n'est ménagé. Les imprécations prophétiques s'appliquaient directement au peuple actuel. . . ." (*L'Inspiration biblique*, p. 77). See Soulié for extensive treatment of this topic.

Je suis entre les morts transi,
Franc & quitte de ceste vie
  Item.
Tes fureurs ont sur moy passé
Tes espouvantemens horribles,
  & c.

Comme ledit presche second estoit achevé, & le pseaume sus mentioné se chantoit, voici, apres quelques pierres ruees contre l'assemblee, une esmeute de peuple, qui lors accompagnoit une procession qui se faisoit tout exprés, laquelle se jettant sur l'assemblee, qui estoit belle, d'une furie extreme, eust assomé toute la troupe, si ce bon Dieu, n'esut susscité quelques soldats estrangers. . . .[26]

The prophetic ministry of the pastor is clearly seen in the way in which these two ministers found themselves as if by divine direction edifying the congregation with two biblical texts—the Gospel of Mark and Psalm 88— that spoke directly to their own circumstances. Of the two texts, Tousssain focuses almost exclusively on the psalm. The reason for this is seen in his conclusion to the narrative:

Mais ce qui est avenu à diverses fois aux fideles d'Orleans & a continué un long temps est bien suyvant ce qui fut là chanté en la derniere assemblee comme il a esté dict cy dessus du pseaume 88. Seigneur toutes tes fureurs ont passé pardessus moy.[27]

Toussain found a complete conformity between the original situation of the psalm and that of his congregation, and the psalm therefore summed up for him the history of the Church of Orléans.

Toussain's narrative is a striking example of the type of personal appropriation of Scripture in general and the psalms in particular that was at the heart of Huguenot faith. The French Confession of Faith of 1559 gives a clear formulation of this approach to Scripture:

---

[26] Daniel Toussain, *L'Exercise de l'ame fidele, assavoir Prieres et Meditations pour se consacrer en toutes sortes d'afflictions*, MDLXXXII, pp. 7r–8r. This passage is typical of the *L'Exercise* as a whole, which, as Barbara B. Diefendorf says, is "studded with passages from the psalms, all cited with the purpose of reassuring the faithful that God will not abandon those whom he has called to share in the inheritance of Christ. Toussain cites passages from other books of the Bible as well, but the most numerous references are to the Book of Psalms, which delivers the reassuring message in familiar terms" ("The Huguenot Psalter and the Faith of French Protestants," in *Culture and Identity in Early Modern Europe [1500–1800]. Essays in Honor of Natalie Zemon Davis*, ed. Barbara B. Diefendorf and Carla Hesse [Ann Arbor: The University of Michigan Press, 1993], p. 51).

[27] Toussain, *L'Exercise de l'ame fidele*, p. 9v.

> Cela se fait d'autant que les promesses de vie qui nous sont données en lui [Christ] sont appropriées à notre usage, et en sentons l'effet quand nous les acceptons, ne doutant point qu'étant assurés par la bouche de Dieu, nous ne serons point frustrés. Ainsi la justice que nous obtenons par foi dépend des promesses gratuites par lesquelles Dieu nous déclare et testifie qu'il nous aime.[28]

Although the specific issue at hand in this passage is justification by faith, its principle extends to all aspects of the Christian life, especially because justification by faith was one of the fundamental notions of Protestant doctrine. The basic principle is that of appropriation of the Bible. For the authors of this confession—and by extension for the believers in whose name they wrote—the Christian life is realized as each one comes to Scripture, understands its teachings, and appropriates them personally. As such, Protestant Bible reading was a very rational act establishing a direct and immediate relationship between mankind and God through the Word.[29] As one of the statements of faith of the times says, "We are established by the Word of God"; the Church of Orléan's appropriation of Psalm 88 is what established them in their identity as God's people and gave them assurance in the midst of their trials.

This type of direct appropriation of Scripture is really what constituted the originality of Protestantism, which explains why Catholics reacted to it as an embodiment of heresy. The Huguenot use of the psalms proved to be a very important issue during the Religious Wars. As early as 1543 the Sorbonne had condemned the Huguenot Psalter "comme contenant damnable et pernicieuse doctrine."[30] Protestant psalm singing was at the center of many prewar incidents—including the massacre of Vassy, which launched the first war—and continued to be a problem throughout the religious conflicts.[31] The following example from an incident at Angers is helpful for understanding exactly what was at issue concerning the psalms:

---

[28] Olivier, *Confessions et cathéchismes*, p. 121.

[29] A similar passage in the Second Helvetic Confession explains it in the following manner: "What is Faith? Christian faith is not an opinion or human conviction, but a most firm trust and a clear and steadfast assent of the mind, and then a most certain apprehension of the truth of God presented in the Scriptures and in the Apostles' Creed, and thus also of God himself, the greatest good, and especially of God's promise and of Christ who is the fulfillment of all promises" (*Reformed Confessions of Faith*, p. 257).

[30] Cited by Henri Chaix, *Le Psautier Huguenot. Sa Formation et son histoire dans l'Eglise Réformée* (Geneva: Imprimerie Romet, 1907), p. 91.

[31] Donald R. Kelley, *The Beginning of Ideology. Consciousness and Society in the French Reformation* (Cambridge: Cambridge University Press, 1981), pp. 97–99.

A Angers . . . ils [les soldats catholiques] prirent dans la maison d'un grand marchand "une grande Bible bien reliée et dorée, la fichèrent au bout d'une hallebarde et firent une procession au travers de toutes les grandes rues, criant et hurlant: 'Voilà la vérité pendue, la vérité des huguenots, la vérité de tous les diables! Voilà 'le Dieu, le Fort, l'Eternel parlera,' et en cette façon étant parvenus jusqu'au pont la jetèrent dans la rivière."[32]

Certainly the Catholic troops were in no way reacting against the Bible itself, for it was also the basis of their faith and they were as devoted to it as their opponents. Rather, they were reacting against the Huguenots' misunderstanding of Scripture and consequent abuse of it. The "Voilà 'le Dieu, le Fort, l'Eternel parlera,'" the first line of Psalm 50, decries the Protestants' appropriation of the psalms and the type of immediate link they claimed to have with God through it. The Catholic expressions of indignation denounced the Protestants' notion of truth: that of claiming the Bible as the unique source of all truth, available for all to apprehend directly without the intermediary of the official Church.

CATHOLIC BIBLE READING AND MEDITATION

The vehemence with which the Huguenots' particular and unique appropriation of the psalms was attacked emphasizes the critical differences between their approach and that of the Catholic Church. The Bible had also, of course, always been central to Catholicism, which is why Catholics reacted so strongly to what they perceived as Protestant abuse of the sacred texts. In response to the Huguenot heresy, the Catholic Church's stand on Scripture was carefully formulated in the decrees of the Council of Trent. In the early sessions of the council, Church leaders reaffirmed the centrality of Scripture for Catholicism:

Orthodoxorum patrum exempla secuta, omnes libros tam veteris quam novi testamenti, cum utriusque unus Deus sit auctor, necnon traditiones ipsas, tum ad fidem tum ad mores pertinentes, tamquam vel oretenus a Christo, vel a Spiritu Sancto dictatas et continua successione in ecclesio catholica conservatas. . . . Si quis autem libros ipsos integros cum omnibus suis partibus, prout in ecclesia catholica legi consueverunt et in veteri vulgata latina editione habentur, pro sacris et canonicis non

---

[32] Quoted by Félix Bovet, *Histoire du Psautier des Eglises Réformées* (Neuchâtel: Librairie Générale de J. Sandoz, 1872), p. 125.

susceperit, et traditiones praedictas sciens et prudens contempserit: anathema sit.[33]

In addition to this reverence for Scripture, there was a very strong emphasis on teaching, similar to that of the Protestants. For example, during the fifth session the following proclamation was made:

> Quia vero Christianae reipublicae non minus necessaria est praedicatio evangeli quam lectio, et decrevit eadem sancta synodus, omnes episcopes, archiepiscopes, primates et omnes alios ecclesiarum praelatos teneri per se ipsos, si legitimi impesiti non fuerint, ad praedicandum sanctum Jesu Christi evangelium.[34]

In other sections of the proceedings of the Council of Trent the importance of preaching in the parish churches is underscored, and the bishops, prelates, and others are admonished to explain the mysteries of the mass and the sacraments to the faithful. Such decrees clearly show that the Bible held an equally important place in the Catholic Church as in the Protestant Church.

It is also clear that the way this importance was expressed and the way the Scriptures were actually used in the Catholic community differed vastly from Protestant practices. In the decrees of the Council of Trent quoted above, it is true that the centrality and eminence of Scripture were reaffirmed, but in a way that presents great differences with Protestant doctrine. For the ecclesiastics at the Council of Trent, Scripture could not be separated from the Church itself and its traditions ("necnon traditiones ipsas . . . continua successione in ecclesio catholica conservatas. . . ."). Herein lies the fundamental difference between Catholics and Protestants concerning the Bible: Catholics believed that the Church had a governing and mediatory role to play regarding the Scriptures. For them, it was a sacred gift to the Church, whose

---

[33] ["Following, then, the examples of the orthodox Fathers, it receives and venerates with a feeling of piety and reverence all the books both of the Old and New Testaments, since one God is the author of both; also the traditions . . . as having been dictated either orally by Christ or by the Holy Ghost, and preserved in the Catholic Church in unbroken succession. . . . If anyone does not accept as sacred and canonical the aforesaid books in their entirety and with all their parts, as they have been accustomed to be read in the Catholic Church and as they are contained in the old Latin Vulgate Edition, and knowingly and deliberately rejects the aforesaid traditions, let him be anathema."] *Canons and Decrees of the Council of Trent* (St. Louis: B. Herder Book Company, 1941), p. 297 [trans. pp. 17–18].

[34] ["But since the preaching of the Gospel is no less necessary to the Christian commonwealth than the reading thereof, and since this is the chief duty of the bishops, the same holy council has ordained and decreed that all bishops, archbishops, primates and all other prelates of the churches are bound personally, if not lawfully hindered, to preach the holy Gospel of Jesus Christ."] *Canons and Decrees*, p. 305 [trans. p. 26].

ministers alone had the responsibility and ability to teach its truths to the laity.[35] Whereas Protestants considered accessibility and applicability to be the most important aspects of the divine writings, Catholics focused more on the sacred and lofty nature of the Bible, which they believed required special care.

Consequently, Catholic leaders were opposed to the widespread use of vernacular translations. They thought that such translations were dangerous for unlearned laymen and could be permitted for certain people only at the discretion of the bishop.[36] Because much of the Bible was considered beyond the average layman, which is why it was believed dangerous to let the simple believer have too close a contact with it, the text was left in the official Latin, and the ecclesiastics had the responsibility of explaining some of the elements and mysteries of mass and the sacraments to the congregation (only those necessary for their understanding). As a result, the "simple fidele's" contact with the Scriptures was often once removed, coming necessarily through the Church and its ministers. Roger Chartier sums up well the striking differences between this stance and the views of Protestant reformers:

> L'absence d'un rapport intime et réitéré avec la Bible crée ici une différence fondamentale. . . . En terre catholique, les clercs sont les intermédiaires obligés entre la Parole divine at les fidèles, et aucun livre n'y a une importance existentielle semblable à celle de la Bible chez les réformés, la Bible dont la présence dans chaque famille est vérifiée, dont le texte connu par coeur après de multiples auditions et lectures est souvent récité à soi-même.[37]

Simply put, as a result of the Church's official stand on Scripture, most Catholics did not have the same type of close contact with the Bible as their Huguenot counterparts.

That is certainly not to say, however, that Catholic spirituality was any less intense. Catholics simply had a different relationship with the Bible, and the type of interaction they had with the sacred texts is reflected in Catholic devotional works. The production of such works was extremely

---

[35] Because the priests embodied this doctrine of the Catholic Church, much of the Protestant violence during the Religious Wars was directed against them.

[36] "Cum experimento manifestum sit, si sacra biblia vulgari lingua passim sine discrimine permittantur, plus inde ob hominum temeritatem detrimenti quam utilitas oriri, hac in parte judicio episcopi aut inquisitoris stetur, ut cum consilio parochi vel confessari bibliorum a catholicis auctoribus versorum lectionem in vulgari lingua eis concedere possint, quos intellexerint ex hujusmodi lectione non damnun, sed fidei atque pietas augmentum capere posse; quam facultatem in scriptus habeant" (*Canons and Decrees*, pp. 546–47).

[37] Roger Chartier, "Du Livre au lire," in *Pratiques de la lecture*, sous la direction de Roger Chartier (Marseilles: Rivages, 1985), p. 77.

vast.[38] From 1445 to 1520—that is, before the Reformation—for example, 75 percent of all printed works were of a religious nature, and although the percentage did not remain as high throughout all the sixteenth century, it was high nonetheless.[39] Although the nature of the Catholic devotional texts varied widely, a very large proportion of them dealt with meditation or contemplation, which, as seen above, was of major importance throughout the century. One of the best examples of the salient characteristics of Catholic meditation is Ignace de Loyola's *Exercices Spirituels*. The text itself is not a meditation, but rather a guide for spiritual leaders to help others in their search for God. In the annotations at the beginning of the work, the author explains:

> Par le mot même d'exercices spirituels on comprend toute façon d'examiner sa propre conscience, et aussi de méditer, de contempler, de prier mentalement et vocalement, et enfin de mener toutes autres activités spirituelles. . . .[40]

Thus, although meditation does not constitute the whole of the *Exercices*, it does play a central role in the spiritual journey proposed in the work. Because this work was highly influential on Catholic spirituality during the sixteenth century, examining the type of meditations it proposes helps one to understand the major traits of Catholic meditation of that period.

The first characteristic of Catholic meditation is that it was to be done according to a rather formal framework. In the *Exercices*, the way in which the meditator is to proceed is highly structured by the text, which proposes a program of meditation for four weeks. A good example of this is the first day of the second week:

> —Première méditation: L'Incarnation de Jésus-Christ. Elle comprend la prière préparatoire, trois préludes et trois points avec un colloque.
> —La prière préparatoire ne diffère en rien des précédentes.
> —Le premier prélude est d'évoquer l'histoire du sujet à contempler. . . .
> —Le deuxième a pour objet la composition du lieu. . . .
> —Le troisième contient la demande d'une grâce. . . .

---

[38]As Denis Pallier points out, "L'Eglise romaine se montre défavorable aux traductions, tant des Ecritures que des textes patristiques. Pour la célébration de le messe et l'administration des sacrements, elle consacre l'emploi du latin. A l'inverse, la diffusion de la littérature spirituelle repose sur une politique de traduction systématique" ("Les réponses catholiques," in *Histoire de l'édition française. Tome I: Le Livre conquérant* [Paris: Promodis, 1982], p. 334).

[39] Ibid., p. 327.

[40] Saint Ignace de Loyola, *Exercices Spirituels*, trans. Jean-Claude Guy (Paris: Editions du Seuil, 1982), p. 51.

—Il faut noter ici que et la prière préparatoire et les trois préludes se font de la même façon pendant toute cette semaine et les suivantes, en variant pourtant les préludes selon la diversité des sujets. . . .

—J'ajouterai pour finir un colloque, avec des mots choisis avec soin pour me permettre de m'adresser comme elles le méritent à chacune des personnes divines. . . .[41]

Everything is clearly formulated; the exercitant knows exactly what to do when. This type of structure, which is ubiquitous in contemplative texts of the times, reflects the deep concern of Catholic leaders for those under their care. By proposing such structured programs, they endeavored to make these exercises profitable for all, especially for those not accustomed to the discipline required for effective meditation.

As for the subject matter of the meditations, they center mainly on Christ.[42] The meditator is invited to contemplate the life, ministry, sufferings,

---

[41] Ibid., pp. 85–86. In his book, *La Méditation selon l'esprit de Saint Augustin* (Paris: Desclée de Brouwer, 1935), pp. 87–89, Fulbert Cayré presents the following outline of the Ignatian method:

Méthode Ignatienne (d'après les exercices spirituels et les commentateurs)

Préparation immédiate:
   a) oraison préparatoire pour diriger l'intention.
   b) prélude:
      1) composition du lieu et détermination du sujet.
      2) prière pour demander le fruit pratique à prévoir dès maintenant.
Corps de la méditation:
   a) 1er point: lecture présentant le sujet (mystère de la vérité à méditer).
      1) Développement ordinaire par
         —la mémoire: fixer le sujet d'ensemble, dans les grands traits.
         —l'intelligence: en voir la vérité, les raisons et les conséquences.
         —la volonté: s'exciter à aimer celles-ci et les vouloir.
      2) Autres développements, si le sujet s'y prête: ou par application des cinq sens, ou par contemplation (attention aux personnes, paroles, et actions).
   b) 2ème point: mêmes actes.
   c) 3ème point: mêmes actes encore.
Conclusion:
   a) colloques ou entretiens avec Dieu, Jésus-Christ ou les Saints.
   b) rappel des résolutions prises.
   c) revue de la manière dont on a médité.

[42] The types of written meditations Catholics were used to were not related to the psalms for the most part. Mario Richter's findings concerning the number of titles before 1581 (publication of Bèze's meditations) containing the word meditation are very illuminating in this area. Of the nine works he found, eight are due to Catholic authors, and only two of these eight contain parts dealing with the psalms (neither of the two is a work dealing exclusively with the psalms): Jean Bourgeois, *L'ammortissemennt de toutes perturbations et reveil des mourans, excitant au mespris du monde et preparation à la mort, avec meditations sur les sept psaumes penitentiaux. Plus aucuns oraisons tirees des Psalmes de David*, Douai, 1579; *Les meditations du zelateur de pieté*, Paris, 1571. The other works deal with various subjects: François Barat, *Brieve forme et methode de s'exercer par chaque jour*

and glory of Jesus Christ and how he (meditator) is affected by all of these things. On the first day of the third week of the *Exercices Spirituels*, for example, the exercitant is instructed to focus on Christ's agony in the garden of Gethsemane.[43] The basis for the meditation is the narrative of this scene found in the gospels; Loyola specifies that the meditation is to be carried out "selon le récit." It is not just a question of rereading the biblical text, however. The second part of the meditation includes "examiner le chemin: en pente, plat ou rocailleux; de même à décrire le jardin: telle surface, aspect, genre." Finally, the meditator is to "demander la douleur, les larmes, l'angoisse et les autre peines intérieures de ce genre pour compatir au Christ pâtissant pour moi."[44] In this manner, the reader is invited to enter the biblical text emotionally and sensorially. As Jean-Claude Guy points out: "L'essentiel n'y est plus de réfléchir et de comprendre, mais de regarder et de se laisser illuminer et attirer. Aussi faut-il se rendre présent au mystère à contempler."[45] Thus, in spite of its highly structured nature, the Ignatian method was not characterized by dry, rigid exercises. On the contrary, it called for an extremely high emotional and affective participation, encouraging the meditator to picture himself in the scenes of the Bible in order to relive the events in all their emotional intensity and transforming power.

This use of imagination and the senses proposed in the *Exercices* is very different from the type of rational apprehension of the Bible practiced by Protestants and reflects the many mystical elements to be found in Catholic meditations. Although it is true that mysticism in its most intense forms was practiced by a relatively small number of individuals, it nonetheless exercised

---

en la meditation des mystères de la philosophie chrestienne, Paris, 1551; Michel Coyssard, *Les méditations sur la passion de N.S. Jésus-Christ, avec l'art de méditer. Mises en françois de l'italien de R.P.G. Loart*, Paris, 1578; Pierre Doré, *La meditation devote du bon chrestien sur le saint sacrifice de la Messe*, Paris, 1544; Claude d'Espence, *Paraphrases ou meditations sur l'oraison dominicale*, Lyon, 1547; François Grandin, *Meditations de Sainte Brigide reduites en quinze oraisons et traduictes en françois par F.G.*, Paris, 1575; Maurice Poncet, *Meditations familieres sur l'histoire de l'incarnation du fils de Dieu. . . .*, Reims, 1574. These texts show that although Catholics were no strangers to prose meditations, their tradition of this type of meditation was not at all linked with the verse-by-verse exposition of the psalms. Cf. Mario Richter, "A propos des 'Chrestiennes Méditations' de Théodore de Bèze. Essai de définition," in *La Méditation en prose à la Renaissance*, Cahiers V. L. Saulnier, no. 7 (Paris: Presses de l'Ecole Normale Supérieure, 1990), p. 66.

[43] Subjects from the second week include "L'Incarnation de Jésus-Christ," "la nativité," and "la présentation du Christ au Temple." From the third week: "Sur ce que fit le Christ après la cène et au jardin" and "l'histoire depuis le retour de chez Hérode jusqu'à la première moitié des mystères qui se sont déroulés chez Pilate." The fourth week includes "Comment le Seigneur après la Résurrection apparut a sa sainte Mère" and "tous les mystères de la Résurrection et de l'Ascension et ceux qui les séparent."

[44] Loyola, *Exercices Spirituels*, p. 107.

[45] Jean-Claude Guy, introduction to *Exercices Spirituels*, p. 33.

a very strong influence throughout the whole sixteenth century. Mystical elements were already at work in many devotional texts of the early sixteenth century,[46] and, after around 1570—the beginning of the period commonly referred to as the "invasion mystique"—these mystical tendencies became more pronounced. The leaders of the Counter-Reformation found that certain elements of the mystical tradition were helpful for establishing a more intimate and affective element in Catholic devotional practices. As a result, there was an increase in the number of editions of both the northern and Spanish mystics, as well as of original works influenced by them.[47] Like the *Exercices Spirituels*, these texts invite the reader into a mystical union with Christ though visual and emotional contemplation. For example, the *Discours tres proffitable a tous amateurs des graces de la vie Contemplative* of 1586 teaches—through the narrative of the "extase" of a Portugese nun—a path of transformation into God's image through the contemplation of his glory.[48] Another example is Pontus de Tyard's *Homelies, ou contemplations sur la Passion de nostre sauveur Jesus Christ*, which teaches a "force" that comes from a "chastiement et mortification contre son corps, et par devote contemplations et interieures afflictions contre son esprit." Tyard's contemplations include, among others, the following images to be relived by the exercitant:

> He bon Jesus: combien souffriez-vous donc? vos mains sallées furent avec indicible douleur attachées à grosses cordes, pour estendre vos bras desja meurtris: et vos pieds firent sortir à gros bouillons le sang tres sainct et tres pur, coulant à ruisseaux pitoyables le long du bois de vostre Croix sacrée.[49]

Here, as opposed to the splendor of God that the *Discours tres proffitable* proposes for contemplation, the reality of Christ's suffering is supposed to lead the meditator into similar suffering that will help purify him. In either case, the goal is the same: a purification of sinful man through a contemplation of Christ or God, which helps the believer conform to God's image and consequently draws him into union with the divine being.

---

[46] Such as the *Orloge de devocion* of 1500, the *Theologie spirituelle* of 1520, and the French version of the *Contemplations Idiotae* of 1535.

[47] Pallier, "Les résponses Catholiques," p. 335.

[48] *La Vierge stigmatisée. Miracle nouvellement veu et appreuvé à Lisbonne en Portugal, à une tres devote religieuse de l'ordre de S. Dominique. Comme Jesuchrist nostre Seigneur, souventefois s'est apparu à elle, et luy a donné ces cinq playes et stigmates qu'il receut a la Croix. Discours tres proffitable à tous amateurs des graces de la vie Contemplative, dressé sur la relation des Peres dudit Ordre cy dernier nommez, envoyé de Lisbonne* (Lyon: A la Bible d'Or, 1586).

[49] Quoted by Denis Crouzet, *Les Guerriers de Dieu*, Vol. 2 (Paris: Champ Vallon, 1990), p. 441.

PROTESTANTS AND PROSE PSALM MEDITATIONS

As a result of the Protestants' particular Bible-reading practices, the type of relationship with God developed in Protestant meditations was of a totally different nature. Protestant interaction with the Bible in general and the psalms in particular as described earlier can best be summarized by what Roger Chartier calls a *lecture intense*, which he defines as follows:

> la lecture personnelle se trouve située dans tout un réseau de pratiques culturelles appuyées sur le livre: l'écoute de textes lus et relus à haute voix dans la famille ou à l'église, la mémorisation de ces textes entendus, plus reconnus que lus, leur récitation pour soi ou pour les autres. . . . Cette lecture intense produit l'efficace du livre, dont le texte devient une référence familière, dont les formules façonnent les manières de penser et de dire. Un rapport attentif et déférent lie le lecteur et ce qu'il lit, incorporant dans son être le plus intime la lettre de ce qui a été lu.[50]

It is clear that Protestants' reading of the psalms constituted such a lecture intense, for their whole lives were shaped by this one book; hence, the popularity of prose psalm meditations among Protestants. In 1582, Théodore de Bèze's *Chrestiennes Méditations*, a collection of prose psalm meditations, were published in Geneva. This text served as an inspiration for similar collections of prose psalm meditations by other Protestant authors: Jean de Sponde's *Méditations sur les Pseaumes XIIII. ou LIII. XLVIII. L. et LXII.* of 1588, Philippe du Plessis Mornay's *Meditations chrestiennes sur quatre Pseaumes* of 1591, and d'Aubigné's *Meditations sur les Pseaumes* of 1630.[51] Two Catholic authors also published such collections: La Ceppède's *Imitations des pseaumes de la penitence de David* of 1594 and Du Vair's *Meditation sur les Pseaumes de la penitence de David* and *Meditation sur sept Pseaumes de la consolation de David* of 1603. The fact that these Catholic authors wrote such meditations obviously precludes the conclusion that this type of meditation was a uniquely Protestant phenomenon. There is, nonetheless, a certain striking character about the Protestant texts that sets them apart, undoubtedly due to the fact that, because of their intimate acquaintance with and attachment to the psalms, Protestant authors felt more "at home" in these meditations.[52] In addition,

[50] Chartier, "Du Livre au lire," p. 70.

[51] Other devotional works often had one or more meditations on psalms attached at the end of the work, but the present study deals only with collections of meditations devoted entirely to the psalms. The conclusions made concerning these collections, however, also apply to the meditations found in other works.

[52] Jeanneret says: "Parmi les méditations françaises inspirées par les psaumes au XVIe siècle, celles des protestants s'imposent à l'attention: outre leur qualité littéraire, elles doivent à une théologie commune et à un milieu homogène une physionomie d'ensemble qui invite à les

Du Vair and La Ceppède's works certainly represent a minor type of meditation in the overall production of meditative texts among Catholics. In other
words, although both Catholic and Protestant authors composed this type of
meditations, they were more prevalent and important in the Protestant
sphere.

Before turning to a definition of the prose psalm meditations, one sees
that the relationship between the *lecture intense* of the Protestants and the
prose psalm meditations becomes clearer when one compares the prose
meditations with verse meditations, the other type of psalm meditations
written in the sixteenth century. Although neither was the exclusive do-
main of one particular confessional group, it is true that the verse meditations were written mainly by Catholics, whereas the ones in prose were
written mainly by Protestants. Jeanneret describes the main difference between the two forms:

> Bien plus clairement que tout à l'heure [verse meditations], il s'agit, à
> partir d'une suggestion fugitive empruntée au psautier—ou à quelque
> autre livre des Ecritures—, de créer une oeuvre indépendante; l'ambi-
> tion de traduire, de se situer dans une perspective historique, s'efface
> entièrement devant le désir de prêcher ou de donner forme à une ex-
> périence personnelle.[53]

The prose form is thus characterized by a certain liberty with the biblical text.
This liberty, however, must be correctly understood. It is not a liberty, as
Jeanneret's description might suggest, to use the text as a pretext for something unrelated (for the most part, at least); rather, it is a liberty to take the
text and to explore all its possible applications to the different domains of life,
which corresponds to the Protestant notion of the appropriation of Scripture.[54] In essence, then, the use of prose connotes a deeper appropriation of
the Other's discourse, for in the prose meditations the psalmist's words are
applied directly to the life of the meditator.

The particular nature and role of the prose meditations in the sixteenth-
century context is better understood by applying Bakhtin's categories of the
representation of the Other's discourse to the use of the psalms during the

---

considérer comme un tout" (*Poésie et tradition biblique*, p. 403). He speaks only briefly of La Ceppède's and Du Vair's texts, and he finds the latter "un peu plate" in comparison with some of the
Protestant texts. In "A propos des 'Chrestiennes Meditations' de Théodore de Bèze," Mario Richter deals only with the Protestant authors.

[53] Jeanneret, *Poésie et tradition biblique*, p. 401.

[54] Speaking of the French Protestants' affinity for the psalms, Diefendorf says: "The language
of the Psalms was too powerful to be confined to verse form" ("The Huguenot Psalter," p. 45).

Renaissance.[55] The literary appropriation of the psalms in the sixteenth century can be divided into three categories: paraphrases, meditation, and original poetry.[56] The psalm paraphrases illustrate the linear discourse, especially in their nature as a translation of the biblical texts. The original poetry, on the other hand, which is how Jeanneret characterizes the penitential poetry (mainly Catholic) that began to flourish in France around 1570, is representative of the picturesque discourse, in that with it "Nous franchissons . . . un pas de plus: la poésie penitentielle, où le chrétien avoue ses fautes et implore le pardon divin, est une création originelle qui s'inspire à des sources très diverses."[57] Meditation thus occupies a position of tension between the two types of discourse, and this is much more the case for the prose form than for the verse form, which, because of its "less independent" nature, actually leans much more toward the linear end of the spectrum. As for the prose psalm meditations, on the one hand, they are still within the limits of the linear discourse, insofar as they remain explicitly attached to the Hebrew poems. On the other hand, however, the liberty of application and appropriation involved would seem to place them within the range of the picturesque discourse. This ambivalence of the prose form allowed the authors and readers to experience the maximum amount of liberty with the psalms, while still respecting the centrality and importance of the biblical text itself.

A definition of these meditations shows the way this tension played itself out in the texts. As seen above, the genre of meditation in general is not easily defined. However, the task is somewhat less formidable for the prose psalm meditations in particular, because they constitute a small group representing a "certaine évolution dans le genre bien connu de la méditation,"[58] or, as Mario Richter has described it, variations on a certain model proposed within the general framework of meditation.[59] If one defines a

---

[55] According to Bakhtin, there are two basic extremes in reported speech. The first he calls the linear style, characterized by a linear representation of the other's words, which are often reported in direct discourse. The other extreme is called the pictorial style, characterized by a greater "digestion" of the Other's words, which are more often reported in indirect discourse. See Mikhaïl Bakhtine, *Le Marxisme et la philosophie du langage*, trans. Maris Yaguello (Paris: Editions de Minuit, 1977.) (The English translation of this text has been attributed to Voloshinov, a colleague of Bakhtin: V. N. Voloshinov, *Marxism and the Philosophy of Language*, trans. Ladislav Matejka and I. R. Titunik [New York: Seminar Press, 1973]. The quotes from Bakhtin in the present text have all been taken from the English version. Therefore, subsequent references to the book will be designated by "Bakhtin/Voloshinov" followed by the page number of the English edition.)

[56] These categories are presented by Jeanneret, *Poésie et tradition biblique*, p. 418.

[57] Ibid., p. 418.

[58] Ibid., p. 411.

[59] Richter, "A propos des 'Chrestiennes Méditation.'" p. 65.

genre basically as a group of works sharing a common content, form, and style, it follows that the best way to "define" this model or stage of evolution of the genre is to describe the major characteristics of these three areas for this group of texts. Of the three, the first is the most obvious and requires little explanation: although the interpretations and applications differ from author to author they are always based on the Hebrew poems. The questions of form and style, on the other hand, are more complicated; each author has his own distinct manner of treating the biblical material. However, as a result of the authors' similar intentions and goals, and the inherent relationship between the content, form, and style, one does find some basic characteristics that are common to most of the prose psalm meditations: (1) development following the verses of the psalm, (2) use of biblical imagery, (3) use of the language and technique of prayer, (4) use of the language and techniques of sermons, (5) the universality of the Davidic "je," and (6) use of other biblical texts. A brief description of each of these aspects will give a comprehensive understanding of the primary elements of the prose psalm meditations.

1. Development Following the Verses of the Psalm

The first aspect, the development of the meditation following the verses of the psalm, constitutes the fundamental structure of the work, and, as such, is one of the clearest indications of the relationship between the two texts. The basic scheme is rather simple. The author begins with a general introduction that leads more or less naturally to the first verse of the psalm, although sometimes the meditation begins directly with the first verse, which is either directly quoted in full or in part, or paraphrased. Often some kind of textual marker, such as italicized letters or a preceding asterisk, is used in order to separate the verse from the rest of the meditation. Once cited, the verse is developed and commented upon in a variety of ways, the most notable of which will be discussed below (prayer, sermon, development of images, etc.). In whatever manner the author exploits the virtual teachings and applications of the verse, he eventually leads into the next verse and then begins the whole process again. The application of this scheme varies from author to author. La Ceppède, for example, often follows the psalm so closely and amplifies the text so little that his meditation seems to be little more than a prose paraphrase. His development of verses 2–5 of Psalm 6

Éternel! ne me punis pas dans ta colère, et ne me châtie pas dans ta fureur. Aie pitié de moi, Éternel! car je suis sans force; Guéris moi,

Éternel! car mes os sont tremblants. Mon âme est toute troublée; Et
toi, Éternel! jusqu'à quand? . . .[60]

is as follows:

Mon Dieu, ne me recherchez plus courroucé; ne déchargez plus sur moy
vos chastimens judiciaires; ayez pitié de mon infirmité; oeilladez mes
sanglantes playes, et leur appliquez le baume de vos éternels miséricordes.
Hé! qu'attendez-vous plus? jusques à quand vous verray-je irrité?[61]

Jean de Sponde, on the other hand, is often so elaborate in his developments
and digressions that the biblical text becomes lost in his own production. For
the most part, however, the authors proceed in such a way as to maintain a
balance between the psalms themselves and their own developments of them.

2. Use of Biblical Imagery

Following the verses of the psalms almost necessarily involved developing
not only the spiritual teaching of the text, but also the imagery used to con-
vey the biblical message. The highly picturesque nature of Hebrew poetry
and the Jewish notion of the inseparable nature of "spiritual" and "natural"
truth that is so evident in the psalms (e.g., unconfessed sins result in physical
troubles), provided a veritable treasure of images to be exploited by the meditation authors. Although the degree of use and the role of these images in
the meditations differs from author to author—some systematically employ-
ing them, others doing so less frequently—it is a characteristic found at some
points at least in all the works. Sometimes the author merely gives a brief
paraphrase of the image presented in the psalm, without necessarily trying to
add anything to it in any way; elsewhere the images are reformulated and am-
plified, as in Du Vair's version of verses 1–3 of Psalm 6:

Donques avant que vostre fureur se live contre moy, et que vous veniez
avec un juste desdain pour me perdre et ruyner, entendez les humbles
sousplis que mon coeur sousy de peur vous addresse, et recevez ceste
vox faiblette et halettante, qui toute esploree s'escrie ainsi à vous.[62]

The chastening of the Lord becomes "perdre et ruyner," and the "sans force"
and the "os tremblant" and "âme troublée" are seen in the "coeur saisy de

---

[60] This and all subsequent Bible quotations in French, unless otherwise stated, are from the
Nouvelle Édition de Genève, 1979.

[61] Jean de La Ceppède, *Meditations sur les Psaumes*, in *Les Theorèmes, suivis de Imitation des
Psaumes de la penitence* (Toulouse: Colmiez, 1612), p. 8.

[62] Guillaume Du Vair, *Meditations sur les Psaumes*, in *Les Oeuvres du Sieur du Vair* (Paris: Guillaume Loyson, 1618), p. 842.

peur" and the "vox faiblette et halettante." In addition, the images are sometimes repeated, drawn out, and used by the author to present a teaching not
necessarily present in the biblical text itself. The most flagrant example of
such a use of the images is d'Aubigné's meditation on Psalm 133, where the
"bord du sacré vestement" of the psalm becomes the "le peuple bas" and "la
tiare le type du roi." This extreme use of the images of Psalm 133, along with
the others mentioned above, demonstrate a few of the many possibilities that
the psalmic images presented to the meditation authors.

3. Use of the Language and Techniques of Prayer

The important role that prayer plays in these psalm meditations is a reflection of the close relationship that has always existed between the two in
Christian spirituality. Strictly speaking, prayer and meditation are two separate things, meditation being an act of reflection within the believer's spirit,
essentially addressed to himself. For this reason, the meditator often directly interpellates part of himself (his soul, spirit, or conscience) in the text
of the meditation, as in the following passage from Bèze's meditation on
Psalm 6:

> Pourquoi donc te troubles-tu, poure conscience? La corruption en
> laquelle tu es, est effacée en ce Sainct des Saincts, conceu, et né pour
> toy: l'obeissance de l'agréable remplit de la plenitude de son obeissance
> jusques'à regorger ce defaut de justice que ton createur requiert de toy:
> les souffrances du Juste des Justes sont ton acquit.[63]

Such "interior conversations" vividly represent the nature of meditation: a
deep reflection on the meaning of a text and its implications (here the efficacy
of Christ's sacrifice) and its application to the life of the believer. In this example, the understanding and full acceptance of the forgiveness available in
Christ are enough to calm the troubled conscience.

For the Huguenots, the nature of biblical teaching was such, however, that
its appropriation necessarily involved more than an understanding and acceptance of abstract ideas. Because the Bible was considered God's Word—that
is, the self-revelation of a person and not a theory—any interaction with it
leads to an interaction with its "sender." Thus, Bèze's meditation on Psalm 6
continues in the following manner:

> Je suis venu à toy, ô Eternel, mon juge et ma partie, j'ay tout confessé, je
> n'ay rien teu, ne desguisé de mon iniquité, et comme je l'avois arresté en

---

[63] Bèze, *Chrestiennes Méditations*, pp. 62–63.

moy, ainsi ay-je fait: me condamnant, j'ay trouvé absolution: et me faisant mon procès, j'en suis sorti.[64]

In this statement one sees the expression of thanks to God for the truth of forgiveness, because God is the one who had been offended and who nonetheless offered pardon. This example illustrates the wholly natural relationship that exists between prayer and meditation; it would seem impossible to reflect on the meaning and applications of the biblical texts without being driven to communication with their author. In fact, not doing so would invalidate the final goal of the meditation, which is always meant to bring the meditator into a deeper relationship with God. As a result, prayer forms an integral part of the process of meditation and is thus found at every point in the prose psalm meditations.

One place where prayer often intervenes in the meditations is at the beginning of the text, where the author invokes God's guidance in the spiritual exercise. Bèze, for example, begins his meditation on Psalm 51 in the following manner:

O Dieu qui nous met devant les yeux en une mesme personne de David un vrayement merveilleux exemple de péché, et de repentance, et de tes compassions, fay moy entendre et bien considerer ses regrets pour les appliquer à mon usage et à ta gloire.[65]

In addition, at various points throughout the meditations there is an outpouring of either self-condemnation for falling short of God's glory, a praise of a certain aspect of God's character or of one his mighty deeds, or thanksgiving. d'Aubigné, for example, addresses the following prayer to God in his meditation on Psalm 73:

Nous confessons donc, o Dieu, que nous t'avons offensé en nos pensees, quand nous avons mesuré tes jugemens à nostre aulne, estimé tes verges à deffaveur, et la prosperité mondaine à felicité.[66]

Finally, the meditation often ends in a sort of apotheosis, as seen in the conclusion to d'Aubigné's meditation on Psalm 51:

Et quand il te plaira nous faire dignes d'estre nous mesmes immolés, pour le tesmoignage de ta verité et de ton nom, nettoye-nous, Seigneur, des taches qui nous rendent impropres à tes offertes. Ren nous par

---

[64] Ibid., p. 63.
[65] Ibid., p. 72.
[66] Agrippa d'Aubigné, *Les Méditations sur les Pseaumes*, in *Oeuvres*, ed. Henri Weber (Paris: Gallimard, 1969), p. 532. All subsequent page references to the *Meditations* will be given in parentheses in the text.

cett'hysope nettoyante victimes blanches. Nous serons bien heureux, quand il te plaira prendre nos esprits et nos vies, pour en sacrifice de bon odeur faire fumer ton temple et ton autel. (P. 494)

4. Use of the Language and Techniques of Sermons

God is not the only "Other" to whom the psalm meditations are addressed; they are also addressed to other people, which is the fundamental point of comparison between meditation and sermon, for, as Jean Mesnard points out, a sermon is first and foremost a "discours pour l'autre."[67] The writing and publication of the private spiritual exercise that is a meditation imply that it is no longer meant to be only a private act of worship and communication between author and God, but rather has been opened up and offered to another. In fact, one must wonder to what degree the psalm meditations were ever "pure"—that is, undertaken only for the sake of the author—because they were often written expressly for public consumption. (That is not to deny or question the sincerity and depth of the meditations; rather, it helps to appreciate better the important relationship between meditation and sermon seen in these texts.) The meditations are often dedicated or offered as a whole (either the whole of the collection of meditations, or the whole of a single meditation) to someone, the person usually being named in a dedicatory preface or epistle. Bèze dedicates his work to Anne de Bacon, d'Aubigné to various people, Sponde to Henry IV, and La Ceppède to Mme Louise D'Ancesvne. Such dedications were, of course, a common practice of the times, but that in no way means that it was necessarily devoid of all true meaning. Indeed, in each case the devotion and sincerity of the author would seem to assure a genuine presentation of his work for the spiritual guidance and enrichment of the reader. In this manner, the "original" personal spiritual exercise of the author does not become merely a cold text to be passively read by another, but rather invites the reader to have a similar experience, either by assuming the author's meditation as his own or by undertaking such an exercise on his own with another text. In either case, the goal of the meditation resembles that of a sermon inasmuch as the author hopes that the reader's contact with the text will lead him into a deeper relationship with God.

The relationship between meditation and sermon goes beyond the general similarity of being directed toward another with the goal of strengthening his or her spiritual life (which could be considered only a superficial resemblance);

---

[67] Jean Mesnard, "Introduction," in *La Méditation en prose à la Renaissance*, Cahiers V. L. Saulnier, no. 7 (Paris: Presses de l'Ecole Normale Supérieure, 1990), p. 12.

the meditation authors also employ sermon techniques in the development of their works. The most obvious "technical" similarity is that both meditation and sermon are usually based on a specific biblical text that is explained and elucidated. Moreover, the relationship goes one step further in as much as the means by which this is done are basically the same; as Terence Cave has noted, both meditation and sermon involve "argument and persuasion, illustration and analysis."[68] This adoption of sermonic methodology in the psalm meditations seems to be the result of two fundamental factors. First, as Cave points out, for Calvinists "meditation is an adaptation to private devotion of sermon-technique—text, debate, apostrophe, and prayer. . . ."[69] Thus, often in these texts the self is treated as another who must be taught, convinced, encouraged, rebuked, and upbraided. This is directly related to the introspective, personal nature of meditation discussed earlier, and the quote taken from Bèze's meditation on Psalm 6 amply illustrates some of the sermonlike qualities of meditation. The "Pourquoy donc te troubles-tu, povre conscience?" is a poignant example of an emotionally charged apostrophe that conveys both a sympathetic understanding and identification (as the pastor who addresses his congregation as one of them) as well as a desire to "shake up" his soul with such a query, to make it question its present attitude and to prepare it for the message that is to follow. The message is one of hope and encouragement based on a christological analysis and interpretation of Psalm 6, expressed in such a way as to convince fully the meditating soul of the practical application of the teaching.

The second factor that accounts for the sermonic nature of the psalm meditations is the climate of confessional division in which they were written. The Reformation and Counter-Reformation context of these works had, of course, a profound impact on both their form and content. Major theological and doctrinal differences thus found their expression in sermonic form in the meditations. During the first half of the century it might have been possible for an author to treat a religious subject without a parti pris concerning the religious problems that were beginning to divide the country. However, during the period when the prose psalm meditations were written, such impartiality was impossible and unthinkable, which resulted in each author trying (overtly or subtly) to convince his reader (and himself?) of his position. Sometimes it comes in the form of a clearly didactic exposition, as in the following example from d'Aubigné's meditation on Psalm 51, where he manages to underline the notion of election:

---

[68] Terence Cave, *Devotional Poetry in France, 1570–1613* (Cambridge: Cambridge University Press, 1969), p. 37.
[69] Ibid., p. 39.

> Mais voici une seconde charité qui surpasse la premiere, que la nation esleuë ayant renoncee ou crucifié le Sauveur et Dieu de Gloire, il a mis la main sur nous, et sans occasion de choix, en ce qui estoit du nostre, nous a tirés d'entre les idolatres courans après les bois et la pierre, pour nous adopter en la place et au rang des enfans d'Abraham. . . . (P. 545)

Elsewhere one finds an amplification of a verse that is obviously meant to serve as a living illustration of just how exactly it should be applied. For example, Du Vair renders verse 7 of Psalm 32 as follows, "Que me restoit-il plus, sinon que ceux que vous approchez pres de vous, & que vous avez receu au sacré consistoire de vostre éternité, vous suppliassent d'avoir pitié de moy?"[70] As a good preacher, Du Vair shows his reader just how this verse should be applied; according to him, this must be interpreted as referring to the Saints. These examples show just a few of the many ways in which the Psalm meditations fulfilled the role of sermon in the lives of the readers.

5. The Universality of the Davidic "je"

Another major characteristic of the psalm meditations is related to all those previously mentioned: the use and role of the first person singular. Because the meditation follows closely the themes and development of the psalms, it is not surprising that the authors chose to retain the Davidic "je" in their own texts. However, it is clear that doing so is not merely a repetition or imitation of the psalms, but rather an important element for the spiritual function of the meditations. Although the use of "je" presents a plethora of possibilities that each of the authors exploits in a variety of ways, it appears to fulfill two major roles. First, there is the notion of witness, a concept deeply woven into the fabric of the Hebrew religion, and thus omnipresent in the psalms themselves. In Psalm 40, for example, David exclaims:

> J'annonce la justice dans la grande assembleée; Voici, je ne ferme pas mes lres, Eternel, tu le sais! Je ne retiens pas dans mon coeur ta justice, je publie ta vérité et eon salut; Je ne cache pas ta bonté et ta fidélité dans la grande assemblée. (vv. 9–10)

This is indeed one of the underlying themes of the psalms: a personal proclamation of God's actions in the life of the psalmist; that is, a personal testimony. The repetition of "je" in the meditations prolongs this notion of testimony on two levels. First, on the most basic level, it carries on David's personal testimony through direct quotation, paraphrase, simple allusion, etc. Thus Bèze

---

[70] Du Vair, *Meditations sur les Psaumes*, p. 847.

can call David a "vrayment merveilleux exemple." However, the witness is not only that of the original psalmist, but also becomes that of the author of the meditation, who in principle has appropriated the psalm for himself and thus uses the "je" to express his own thoughts and feelings. One of the most striking examples of this process is d'Aubigné's meditation on Psalm 8, written after the death of his wife. In one of the most poignant moments of d'Aubigné's work, the Davidic "je" allows him to express his inner torment as he substitutes himself for the psalmist. In offering this meditation to the public, he invited others to observe the working out of faith in the life of one believer, a witness for the reader to his life in Christ.

The use of "je" is not meant, as seen above, to be only a witness, but also to provide an example. In a very general sense, the use of "je" facilitates the reader's assimilation and appropriation of the meditation for himself. The effort needed to assume another person's experience is greatly diminished, because there is no need to make the transition from "he" to "I." As Marie Madeleine Fragonard has said, the use of "je" "permet des autobiographies successives."[71] In other words, each new reader is able to "insert" himself into the discourse of the meditation and apply it to his own life. This is especially evident in all the passages regarding confession and repentance, where the "je" leads the reader into the repentance of his own faults, as in the following passage from La Ceppède's meditation on Psalm 38: "Je passeray ordinairement devant les yeux de ma mémoire mes fautes detestables, et les detestant, les confesseray publiquement pour vostre grandeur et mon ravallement."[72] The importance of this technique is that, as Fragonard clarifies, "[il] permet un discours sur le plus intime de la foi, qui se vit et ne s'enseigne pas."[73] It helps guarantee the transition from a written text to a living reality.

6. Use of Other Biblical Texts

Although the psalm being meditated on is of central interest, another important feature of the psalm meditations is the role played by other biblical texts in the meditations. All of the authors in question freely intersperse either direct quotations, paraphrases, or allusions to other passages of Scripture in their texts. Because all of the authors had a very vast knowledge of the Bible, it was normal and natural for them to link related passages. In addition, it was a basic principle of biblical interpretation that the Bible had to be interpreted

---

[71] Marie Madeleine Fragonard, *La Pensée religieuse d'Agrippa d'Aubigné et son expression*, Vol. 1 (Lille: Atelier National de Reproduction des Thèses, 1986), p. 114.
[72] La Ceppède, *Meditations sur les Psaumes*, p. 15.
[73] Fragonard, *La Pensée religieuse*, p. 116.

as a whole, intertextually. Therefore, there was no better way to clarify and magnify the meaning of the text in question than by relating it to similar passages. This was especially true in relation to other psalms. Fragonard's statement concerning d'Aubigné's work applies to most of the psalm meditations: "un psaume s'éclaire par tous les autres et les éclaire aussi: système de miroirs refermés sur eux-mêmes, ou plutôt sur Dieu, totalité du sens qu'on espère capter."[74] One notable example of such an "illumination" is found in Du Vair's meditation on Psalm 27. Before actually considering the verses of the psalm, he begins with an introduction that uses the theme of Psalm 73. He uses this passage to develop the idea of consolation, which is the theme of the psalm on which he is focusing.

This system of intertextual interpretation did not apply only to the psalms and the rest of the Old Testament; indeed, its application to the New Testament was of utmost importance. The title of Bèze's collection of meditations is most revealing: *Chrestiennes Méditations*. As such, his, and the other meditations, were meant to center on the person and work of Christ and their application to the believer's life. Believing the Old Testament to be the shadow of the New, the meditation authors worked to show how the teachings of the Hebrew Bible found their ultimate fulfillment and meaning in the teachings of and about Jesus Christ in the New Testament. The most obvious application of this christological interpretation of the psalms is the interpretation of the repentance and forgiveness passages in light of Christ's death and resurrection. For Protestants, the New Testament teachings on salvation by faith alone are especially emphasized concerning this issue. However, the influence of New Testament theology is not limited to the notion of forgiveness, but rather is applied to all the aspects of the meditator's life. Thus, d'Aubigné's meditation on Psalm 73 contains the following passage taken from Romans 8:

> mais rien ne me separera de la dilection de Christ, ni oppression, ni angoisse, persecution, famine, nudité, peril, ni espee, estant asseuré que ni mort, ni vie, ni Anges, ni principautés, ni puissances, ni choses presentes, ni àvenir, ni hautesse, ni profondeur, ne pourront aussi nous separer de la dilection de Dieu qu'il nous a monstree en Jesus Christ. (P. 535)

In a meditation meant to bring consolation, d'Aubigné presents the ultimate consolation as the assurance of the love of Christ in all afflictions.

In the end, these prose psalm meditations capture the essence of the personal, direct apprehension of Scripture so characteristic of Protestants. As the

---

[74] Ibid., p. 21.

meditation moves through the psalm verse by verse, bringing in related passages from elsewhere, it leads the meditator to become the psalmist by adopting the biblical "je" for himself. There is much more going on, however, than a simple repetition of the verses of the psalm; by restating the biblical truth through sermonlike exposition and through prayer, the exercitant appropriates these truths in a very personal manner. This humble restatement of the divine Word, which makes it more accessible to the human heart, allows a meaningful interiorization of Scripture. The meditations on Psalm 51, the penitential psalm par excellence that all of the authors treat, very forcefully demonstrates this. Having rejected the Catholic sacrament of penitence as an invention of man, Protestants turned directly to the Bible to repair their relationship with God.[75] By assuming the character of David and expanding the original situation of the psalm to englobe their own circumstances, they found a model for repentance, and, most importantly, the assurance that through their appropriation of this psalm, they were indeed reconciled to God. These meditations were thus a means of being "assuré par la bouche de Dieu," as described in the Confession of 1559.

---

[75] When the Catholic authors wrote meditations on Psalm 51, there was never any question of this taking the place of the sacrament of penitence.

II

"Langage de Canaan":
Language, Myth, and Politics during the
Wars of Religion

The term "en simplicité du langage de Canaan," which d'Aubigné introduces in the preface of the *Meditations*, must be understood in order to comprehend the work. To explore the meaning of the expression, one must first consider both sixteenth-century notions of language in general and d'Aubigné's specific remarks on language in the preface. In addition, it is necessary to understand the importance of Canaan for the Huguenots and to look at the way the spiritual, literary, and political implications of Canaan are manifested in the *Meditations*. Examining the significance of the "langage de Canaan" in this way leads to a fuller comprehension of the form, content, and dynamics of *Les Meditations sur les Pseaumes*.

QUESTIONS OF LANGUAGE IN THE RENAISSANCE

The type of personal appropriation of the language of Scripture found in the prose psalm meditations was an outgrowth of the sixteenth century's preoccupation with language.[76] Although it is true that every century has been preoccupied with language in one way or another—from the medieval debates over the capacity of verse and prose to represent truth to the experiments of the surrealists in the twentieth century—as a result of the "rediscovery" and veneration of ancient texts in the original language coupled with the rise of

---

[76] For a discussion of language in the sixteenth century, see Claude-Gilbert Dubois, *Mythe et langage au XVIe siècle* (Paris: Ducros, 1970); Michel Foucault, *Les Mots et les choses* (Paris: Gallimard, 1966); and Michel de Certeau, *La Fable Mystique* (Paris: Gallimard, 1982).

the vernacular, questions about the importance and role of language were a most pressing concern for Renaissance figures. This was especially true because sixteenth-century thinkers had a "vision synchronique et globale du phénomène linguistique."[77] In other words, language was not an entity existing on its own and separable from the rest of reality. Words and things were inextricably intertwined, and language did not simply represent or signify a world exterior to it but rather actually revealed and expressed the realities it named.[78] Moreover, this understanding and apprehension of the world through language led also to the understanding and apprehension of the divine because, through the profoundly analogical world view of the Renaissance, humans and the physical world around them were considered mirrors of the unseen, spiritual world. In this manner, language was truly an essential element of life, for through it, and only through it, came knowledge of the world and of God.

That is not to say that Renaissance thinkers felt that the particular languages they spoke, be they Latin, French, or English, gave them a true hold on reality. Far from it, in fact; it was well understood that as a result of the Fall and, more specifically, Babel, no single language could capture the world in all of its complexity. Babel was thus the origin of man's linguistic confusion and the reminder of God's curse on humanity, but at the same time it was the reminder of the time before Babel, before the Fall, a time when there was indeed a true correspondence between the referent and the sign. Calvin comments on the first chapter of Genesis:

> chaque espece était venue en la présence d'Adam et il leur avait imposé les noms, non point à la volée, mais par conaissance certaine. . . . Quant aux noms qu'Adam a imposés, je ne doute point qu'il n'y eût tres bonne raison en chacun. Mais leur usage, comme de beaucoup d'autres bonnes choses, est aboli.[79]

Adam's language was one of "connaissance certaine"; language and knowledge were one and the same. Such a language had thus existed in the past, before Babel, and humanity had to deal with the cleavage between its own fallen language and that former, ideal one. One reaction to this situation was the utopian search for the original Adamic language, a dream that haunted much of the sixteenth century.[80]

---

[77] Dubois, *Mythe et langage*, p. 16.

[78] See esp. Foucault, *Les Mots*, chaps. 2–4, pp. 32–136.

[79] Jean Calvin, *Commentaires sur l'Ancien Testament. Tome Premier: Le Livre de la Genèse* (Geneva: Labor et Fides, 1961), p. 58.

[80] See Dubois, *Mythe et langage*, pp. 31–48.

For the most part, however, it was understood that one could not overcome the effects of Babel by trying to reconstruct Adam's lost language; after
all, "retrouver la langue d'Adam, c'est forcer à rebours les portes du Jardin
défendu."[81] Instead, redemption was sought in the very plurality of the existing languages. First, the symbolic function of language was revealed not

> dans les mots eux-mêmes mais bien dans l'existence même du langage,
> dans son rapport total à la totalité du monde, dans l'entrecroisement de
> son espace avec les lieux et les figures du cosmos.[82]

Claude Duret, for example, believed the various ways in which different
peoples write—some right to left or left to right, others top to bottom or
bottom to top, and still others in spirals—signified the totality of the universe
in its physical and spiritual dimensions:

> par ces cinq sortes d'écrire les secrets et mystères de la croisée du monde
> et de la forme de la croix, ensemble de la rotondité du ciel et de la terre,
> sont proprement dénotées et exprimées.[83]

Also, in addition to the truth languages revealed when considered together as
a global phenomenon, the ability to communicate from one language to the
next was also seen as a step in overcoming the effects of Babel:

> il y a une bonté merveilleuse de Dieu qui reluit en ce que les gens com-
> muniquent entre eux de part et d'autre par divers langages, et princi-
> palement en ce qu'il a publié un Evangile par toute la terre en diverses
> langues et a appris à ses Apôtres à parler divers langages; par ce moyen,
> ceux qui auparavant étaient misérablement divisés ont été conjoints par
> l'unité de la foi.[84]

Although, as this passage shows, Calvin and other Reformers like him were
particularly excited about the possibility of spreading the gospel in all languages, his enthusiasm for language in general sums up well the excitement
of the period concerning communication *intra linguas*.[85]

---

[81] Ibid., p. 25.
[82] Foucault, *Les Mots*, p. 52.
[83] Ibid.
[84] Calvin, *Commentaires*, p. 184.
[85] Another testimony of this excitement comes from Ambroise Paré: "nous voyons l'homme
avoir telle dexterité, qu'il ne sçait seulement pas apprendre les divers langages qui sont entre ceux
de son espece, mais aussi apprendre ceux des oiseaux: ce qu'on voit par experience d'aucuns bons
compagnons, qui contrefont tous chants des oiseaux, et la voix de toutes bestes, comme nous
avons dit cy dessus, entendent le jargon de plusieurs autres animaux. . . . Et pour conclusion,
l'Homme est ingenieux, sage, subtil, memoratif, plein de conseil, excellent en condition, qui a esté
fait du souverain Dieu, et luy seul entre tous les animaux a esté orné de raison et d'intelligence, de

Because of the profound links between language and being, the ability to communicate was not a neutral act, and language was also considered intimately linked with one's person, that is, with one's morality. "Nostre langage symbolise ordinairement avec nos moeurs," and "Or advient-il ordinairement que nos langages, tant en particulier comme en général, accompagnent la disposition de nos esprits . . .," is how Estienne Pasquier puts it.[86] It follows, first of all, that the way to better a person was to refine the spoken language, and this was an important aspect of humanist thought. For example, the whole enterprise of the Pleiade could be understood in this light. For these authors, the poet's role in society was a great one, for letters in general and poetry in particular were important in the formation of humans' mind and spirit, and for the Pleiade the progress of poetry was intimately linked to the progress of language.[87] Du Bellay's *Deffence et Illustration de la langue française* of 1549 was a practical manifestation of the concern for the progress of the French language. Second, the language one spoke could be used to condemn some and exalt others. That is actually the context in which Pasquier's remarks, quoted above, were made, for his goal was to prove the inferiority of Italians.[88] In either case, whether language was being used for improvement or condemnation, the underlying assumption was the same: language is an essential part of one's being.

Because the sixteenth century lacked the modern notion of individuality, saying that language was an essential part of one's being meant that language was an essential part of one's being-in-society, and thus language played a central role in politics. This is clearly seen in the way Frenchmen perceived the political turmoil of the Religious Wars. Most were convinced that the abuse of language was the root cause of the problems. One example of this conviction comes from Henri Estienne's *Discours merveilleux de la Vie, Actions & Desportemens de la royne Catherine de Medicis*. For Estienne, Catherine's

---

laquelle tous animaux ont esté privés; et en luy revit une image de l'essence divine, qui ne se trouve en nulle autre creature" (*Des animaux et de l'excellence de l'homme* [Paris: Club Français du Livre, 1954], chap. 26, quoted in Dubois, *Mythe et langage*, p. 26).

[86] Estienne Pasquier, *Choix de Lettres sur la Littérature, la Langue et la Traduction*, ed. Thickett (Geneva: Droz, 1956), p. 88; and *Recherches de la France*, in *Oeuvres choisies* (Geneva: Slatkine Reprints, 1968), pp. 91–92.

[87] Henri Weber, *La Création poétique au XVIe siècle en France* (Paris: Nizet, 1955), p. 111.

[88] The passage from the *Recherches* continues: "l'Espagnol, haut la main, produit un vulgaire superbe et plein de piaffe; l'Allemand, éloigné du luxe, parle un langage fort rude. Et lorsque les Italiens, dégénérant de l'ancienne force du Romain, firent plus profession de la delicatesse que de la vertu, aussi formèrent-ils peu à peu de ce langage mâle romain un vulgaire tout efféminé et mollasse."

power was based on what Timothy Reiss calls a "verbal distortion of political reality"[89]: "ains gouverne tout à l'appetit des passions qui la maistrisent, & ores sous pretexte d'un titre audacieusement usurpé regente et continue à nous fouëtter & bourreler cruellement. . . ."[90] Catherine's words thus did not match the reality of the situation; she was only regent by unjustly taking the title for herself. In addition, according to Estienne, she had Henry III declared an adult earlier than usual so she could rule through him with her words:

> elle le fait Majeur, afin que par ce moyen elle peust gouverner seule au nom du Roy, auquel elle feroit dire & faire tout ce que bon luy sembleroit.[91]

In this manner, Catherine's reign was one of total verbal trickery. Montaigne later summed up the civil wars in similar terms:

> nous advient, ce que Thysidides dict des guerres civiles de son temps, qu'en faveur des vices publiques on les batissait de mots nouveaux plus doux, pour leur excuse, abartidissant et amolissant leurs vrais titres.[92]

The basic accusation is always the same: public order is disrupted through the abuse of language. Consequently, hopes for restoration and healing of the country's wounds were placed in the restoration of a clear, well-defined, and common language.

LANGUAGE AND READER IN THE *MEDITATIONS*

It is only within such a context that d'Aubigné's *Meditations* can be fully understood, for it is in terms of language that he both conceived of his work and presented it to the public. In the preface entitled "L'Autheur au lecteur," he

---

[89] Timothy Reiss, *The Meaning of Literature* (Ithaca, N.Y.: Cornell University Press, 1992), p. 35. Reiss gives an example, similar to Estienne's comments on Catherine de Medicis, from l'Hôpital's *Second discours sur l'estat de France*: "If at this moment you wanted to see the image of confusion and disorder, you would find it clearly painted in that party. To begin with, the duke of Mayenne calls himself Lieutenant General of the Royal State and of the crown of France. This is a great illusion: can there be a Lieutenant, if there is no head? and who is head if not the King? Yet the majority of this party doesn't want any King. As to the State: formerly one heard talk of the States of France, but never of the State: or if one heard it named it was when one said, "The King and his State." In that case the State was named in terms of obedience and not of command: and these madmen place it at the head."

[90] Henri Estienne, *Discours merveilleux de la Vie, Actions & Deportemens de la royne Catherine de Medicis. Mère de François II, Charles IX, Henry III, Rois de France* (Paris: 1663[1574]), p. 4.

[91] Ibid., p. 33. He even goes as far as to blame all of the Religious Wars on Catherine's words, for after the Conspiracy of Amboise, "elle crie première & le plus haut contre ces entrepreneurs. . . . Voilà, comme il appert, la cause du premier trouble qui depuis semble avoir semé tous les autres" (pp. 20–21).

[92] Michel de Montaigne, *Essais*, ed. Pierre Villey (Paris: Presses Universitaires de France, 1978), I, 23, 120 B.

reveals his conception of the work and how it is to be received. He speaks of his views on language in general as well as of the specific type of language the *Meditations* contain and what he hopes this language will achieve. His remarks on language in general come in the middle of a discussion of why he chooses to address God as "tu" instead of "vous":

> Je sçay que l'on s'excuse en la mollesse des langues Françoises, Angloises et Flamandes, ou autres imperfections qu'on fait passer pour loi. J'ay pris plus de plaisir aux anciennes harangues faites aux Rois, et aux poëtes de la volee de Ronsard: (puis qu'il n'y a que du langage) ceux-là parlans à tout ce qu'ils ont voulu séparer du vulgaire, ont pris les termes masles de l'unité. . . ." (P. 494)

Echoes of the common belief in the weaknesses of individual languages since Babel are evident in this passage. Also evident is the fact that d'Aubigné was not among those who would search for some ideal Adamic language in order to solve mankind's communication problems. On the contrary, however difficult it may be to deal with the "mollesse" of these "imperfections," the fact remains that they are all mankind has: "puis qu'il n'y a que du langage." The example of the poets is a case in point: the distinction they wished to make in their poetry between majestic and common people was only possible within the language in which the poetry was composed. Doubtless, as a poet, d'Aubigné shared the Pleiade's concern for improving the French language in order to heighten its poetic and communicative capacities, and he is not saying here that language has to be accepted as is with no effort to work out its imperfections as much as possible. He does insist, however, that human language—imperfect as it may be—is central to communication among people.

d'Aubigné's concern for language in the *Meditations* of course goes beyond mere human considerations. His comments on the weakness of human language show that he was well aware of the problems with a book that claims to be from God while coming to humanity in imperfect languages. Nonetheless, for d'Aubigné there is no doubt that God does speak through the Bible, and he reveals in the preface that his goal is to defend Scripture against the claims of those who are too earthly minded:

> C'est que parmi les corruptions de ce siecle les stupides, qui en leur ig- norance affectee n'ont pensees que terrestres, ou les esprits de vanité qui declament ouvertement contre la Parole de Dieu, la descrient pour estre d'un style grossier, infectans d'un mortel desgoust les oreilles des Grands.Ce langage aussi plein de malice que d'orgueil ne se pouvant combattre par disputes ni remonstrances, pource que les professeurs de

l'Atheisme n'advoüent leur impiété qu'à leurs disciples et complices, j'ay estimé estre à propos de faire voir comment parmi les styles les plus éla-bourés les passages de l'Escriture sont non seulement comme un esmail sur l'or, mais comme des pierreries exquises. . . . (P. 493)

The *Meditations* are thus the author's counterattack on the Atheists. Al-though they "déclament ouvertement" and "descrient," their evil has its sources in darkness and secrecy: "n'advoüent leur impiété qu'à leurs disciples et complices . . .," and in response to this the author proposes to "faire voir," to "faire paroistre au jour"—a simple presentation of the evidence that will si-lence the cries of the ignorant. The contrast is clearly established, and the *Meditations* are seen as a light piercing the darkness of others' ignorance. The author is animated not by selfish pompousness, like the "professeurs de l'Athéisme," but by the need of the moment, the imperative to counter the mis-taken notions of the Atheists, and this will be done not through d'Aubigné's own ingenuity and forcefulness, but rather through a demonstration of the Bible's own inherent qualities. As in *Les Tragiques*, d'Aubigné will only be an instrument, pointing out the true nature of Scripture, which will in and by itself be able to correct the mistaken misconceptions of unbelievers.[93]

In order to quiet the attack on biblical language, d'Aubigné proposes to demonstrate its superiority. He continues:

j'ay estimé estre à propos de faire voir comment parmi les styles les plus elabourés, et dans les discours qui pour le moins sont purgez de barba-rie, les passages de l'Escriture sont non seulement comme un esmail sur l'or, mais comme les pierreries exquises, et relevent le langage le plus eslevé, confirment par axiomes, preuvent par arrest du Ciel, illustrent par exemples, et recreent les esprits qui aiment Dieu par ravissantes lumieres et parfaites beautez. (P. 493)

At first glance one might think that the author is suggesting a sort of stylistic commentary and analysis of biblical passages in order to counter critics' claims that the Bible is written in a style "painful to the ear." However, on closer examination, one sees that d'Aubigné's approach is much more compli-cated than that and involves a complex interaction between style and effect, language and communication of spiritual truth. He begins by speaking of the biblical style in very general, laudatory terms. He presents the Bible as superior

---

[93] In the preface to *Les Tragiques*, one learns that it is not really d'Aubigné who is the author, because "Dieu mesme a donné l'argument." d'Aubigné is in this manner merely a scribe transmit-ting his master's message; the contents of the poem thus reveal God's interpretation of the events of the times, and evil is significantly combatted by revealing its eventual and complete judgment and destruction by God.

in every way, placing it "parmi les styles les plus elabourés, et dans les discours qui pour le moins sont purgez de barbarie . . .," and thus freely admitting that there are other writings in these categories. However, the first two elements of his description show that even within the overall category of elaborate styles, the Bible is incomparable. First, it is like "un esmail sur l'or." The comparison is most likely referring to enamel and gold together, not just to enamel in itself. Hence, the style and language of the Bible are not just gold alone, a precious substance, but gold that has been worked over artistically, gold that shines, better than just plain gold. This idea is further developed in the next comparison: "comme les pierreries exquises." A "pierrerie" is not only a precious stone, but one that has been finished and polished, making it even more valuable. This connotation is intensified by the adjective "exquis," which connotes rarity. With these descriptions d'Aubigné places Scripture in a class of its own.

Although these analogies certainly connote superiority, they are general and do not specify exactly what constitutes this superiority. These remarks contain the same ambivalence toward rhetoric and style on the one hand, and the natural power of Scripture on the other, which characterized St. Augustine, who, as Barbara Lewalski has shown in her *Protestant Poetics*, exercised an important influence on Reformation thinkers.[94] "Pierreries" and "or" both have to do with ornamentation and exterior beauty, obviously referring to the actual writing styles and rhetoric of biblical authors. This was certainly a concern for such an accomplished author as d'Aubigné. However, in what follows he appears to be concerned not with the mechanics of style, but rather with the effects of Scripture. First, he expounds further on the notion already developed in the first two comparisons when he says that the Scripture passages "relevent le langage le plus elevé. . . ." Even the loftiest of discourse is embellished when infused with the Bible; the emphasis here lies not on the beauty of the language itself, but on its valorizing effect. He then continues with three points closely related: "confirment par axiomes, preuvent par arrest du Ciel, illustrent par exemples." These at first seem to be a traditional discussion of style, explaining how the author creates desired effects: he uses axioms, divine judgments, and gives many examples. However, what d'Aubigné is saying here goes far beyond a statement on the types of rhetorical techniques the biblical authors employ. It must be remembered that the subject of the verbs is "les passages de l'Escriture." d'Aubigné is not talking about the authors, but about the Bible itself. The verbs used here are of

---

[94] Barbara Lewalski, *Protestant Poetics and the Seventeenth-Century Religious Lyric* (Princeton: Princeton University Press, 1979), pp. 216ff.

extreme importance. He does not say the Scriptures attempt to do these things, which again would be a comment on the means being used for a specific end. However, the force of "confirment," "preuvent," and "illustrent" is such that it connotes a direct effect on the reader. Things are confirmed to the reader by the axioms presented, the divine judgments given are received as proof, the examples given do illustrate truths for the reader. The reading of Scripture thus always constitutes a performative act, in that it always has an impact on the reader's life: what is spoken of in the Scriptures actually takes place as it is enunciated.

Although "confirment," "preuvent," and "illustrent" deal with man's intellectual and emotional capacities, what comes in the last part of the sentence shows that the effect on the reader goes beyond these realms and enters into that of the spirit: "recreent les esprits." This spiritual recreation is nothing less than a new life given to the believer. This is said to be done by "ravissantes lumieres et parfaites beautez." "Lumieres" and "beautez" are sufficiently abstract nouns to retain the reader in the lofty world of the spirit, while nonetheless referring back to the "esmail sur l'or" and the "pierreries exquises," which were exemplary of the style and discourse of the Bible. In this manner, d'Aubigné establishes a direct link between human language and expression on the one hand and the spiritual realm on the other.

In what follows he further develops this link. d'Aubigné points out that the most prestigious writers, speakers, and preachers do not hesitate to quote the

> authoritez de l'Escriture, mesmes aux termes de la version vulgate, qui est telle que chascun cognoist: sachans que mesmes dans la rudesse de celle-là reluit toujours la Majesté de celui qui prononce, et la richesse qui n'a pas besoin d'artifice, pour ravir à soi les yeux de l'ame et l'admiration des esprits. (P. 493)

In this passage, the author makes clear the relationship that exists between the language of the Bible and activity in the spiritual realm. On the one hand there is the text of the Bible: the Scriptures in a specific version, that of the Vulgate. On the other hand, there is the action in the spiritual world that results from hearing and reading the biblical text: a sort of rapture and enlightenment of soul and spirit. The link between the two is "la Majesté de celui qui prononce"; that is, a person and his attributes. d'Aubigné clearly sees all the different authorial voices of the Bible as unified in the One who speaks through them: God himself, who, when he speaks, makes known who he is. In other words, the essence of his person shines forth in his words. d'Aubigné sums up the strength of this spiritual communication of God's person in the term "majesté," which stands for the sovereignty and overall greatness of

God. It is such that it shines through even in a bad translation, and, more-over, it has a powerful effect on the individual. In his commentary on I Corin-thians, Calvin says, "The Word of the Lord constrains us by its majesty, as by a violent impulse, to yield obedience to it."[95] d'Aubigné's "ravir à soi" con-tains the same notion of a violent impulse. For d'Aubigné, this encounter with God through the biblical text is such that it stirs up both worship and obedience on the part of the reader. God thus communicates himself to man through imperfect human words.

That God communicates with the believer through the Bible was certainly a commonplace for Protestants. Also, that God should communicate even through a bad Latin translation was not all that surprising, for, as seen in Calvin's commentary quoted above, God's goodness was manifested "en ce qu'il a publié un Evangile par toute la terre en diverses langages et a appris à ses Apôtres à parler divers langages." Calvin's emphasis is on the message that comes through the words and not on the words themselves: one signified coming through many signifiers. d'Aubigné, on the other hand, focuses on the necessary relationship between the two: divine self-disclosure and human language.[96] d'Aubigné's concern for language is reinforced in the final para-graph, where he discusses why he chooses "tu" instead of "vous." The issue is really one of interpretation, for God's revelation of himself as a person is from the Bible, and the basic question is if the divine "you" should be rendered as "vous" or "tu." For d'Aubigné, "Vous estes Dieu" is wrong, because God is revealed as "un et seul." "Vous" is also wrong, because its usage is less majestic than that of "Toy." Calling God "vous" thus represents both a theological error and a lack of respect and commitment. Hence, the issue is really of great importance, for the choice of a single word can have vast implications. The "tu/vous" controversy is a striking example of the fact that man's knowledge of and relationship with God is necessarily a matter of language, here specifi-cally the French language with its distinction between "vous" and "tu." For d'Aubigné, language is all there is for communication among men, and be-cause God has chosen to reveal and explain himself through language, it is also a necessary part of divine revelation.[97]

---

[95] Jean Calvin, *Calvin's New Testament Commentaries*, vol. 9: *The First Epistle of Paul to the Corinthians*, trans. J. W. Fraser (Grand Rapids: Eerdmans, 1960), p. 51.

[96] Interestingly enough, d'Aubigné does not mention the Holy Spirit, who, Protestants believed, brings the Scriptures alive for the believer. d'Aubigné's belief in the role of the Spirit is evident in the meditations themselves, and the fact that he does not mention the Holy Spirit spe-cifically in this preface (he does mention the spiritual realm) only highlights his interest in the necessary role of language in spiritual communication. At least in the preface, the fact that one reaches things divine from things human is more important than exactly how this happens.

[97] In arguing his point, Dubois refers to Calvin's commentary on Genesis: "Tout le problème

Nonetheless, not all can understand God's language. Because the language one speaks is intimately linked with one's "moeurs," it follows that atheists would not be capable of receiving God's words. Accordingly, d'Aubigné's proposed that demonstration of the superiority of the Bible actually involves excluding the very people he claims to be targeting. At the very beginning of the preface, the generality of the subtitle *L'Autheur au lecteur* seems to give an open invitation to all, but as the preface progresses it becomes clear that this generality was only apparent. d'Aubigné does indeed directly confront unbelievers and proposes to respond to their ideas and opinions. However, this confrontation is in effect the first step in a move toward a very well-defined group as the ideal readers of the meditations, a group that definitely does not include atheists. The unflattering description of atheists, who are polarized as evil, does not really address them but rather serves to create an "us/them" mentality, and the reader is obviously meant to be one of "us," on the same side as d'Aubigné, with the same distrust of "them." Thus, the response to the atheists is, in reality, a means of establishing a complicity between the author and the like-minded Christian reader.

Indeed, the major invitation in this preface is obviously to d'Aubigné's fellow believers. Applied to this group of readers, the generality of the term "lecteur" would seem to preclude any reference to a certain type of believer, that is, Protestant or Catholic. On closer examination of the text, however, it becomes evident that d'Aubigné is clearly addressing other Protestants, whom he believes are uniquely capable of experiencing the truth that the meditations will reveal. In fact, the first sentence hints at the type of meditations to be found in the work, when d'Aubigné says, "Plusieurs diverses occasions m'ont excité aux meditations que ce Livret vous presente, lesquelles sont specifiees specifiquement en leur place . . ." (493). The meaning of this sentence becomes much clearer to the reader when he actually reads the *Occasions et Arguments* before each meditation, which explain the particular circumstances in which the meditations were written. However, the notion is already established in this preface that the meditations are the response to specific circumstances of the author's or another's life. This type of meditation was doubtless much more familiar to Protestants, as the result of Protestant teaching on the applicability of the Scriptures; as seen in the preceding

---

pour les Protestants . . . consistera à faire le meilleur usage des outils imparfaits qui ont été légués malgré le péché et, en même temps, par le péché: il s'agit de retrouver le sens derrière le signe et sa diversit" (Dubois, *Mythe et langage au XVI*e *siècle*, p. 56). This echoes d'Aubigné's sentiments, but, again, d'Aubigné is less preoccupied with "le sens derrière le signe," than he is with the fact that the "sens" can come *only* through the "signe."

chapter, Catholic meditations were much less spontaneous than the kind of meditation presented in d'Aubigné's "Livret." In this context the generality of "au lecteur" does have a particular significance, for although on certain levels it is somewhat deceptive, it also underlines the possibility of the appropriation of all these meditations by anyone, showing that this type of meditation, which is based on the ability of each individual to meditate on the Bible, is indeed a possibility for all. These connotations of "au lecteur" become even more evident when one recalls that the Psalm meditations of the other Protestant authors all began with dedicatory epistles to specific figures. Although writing such prefaces was often just a matter of following customary procedures and these other authors also clearly meant their works to be received by all, d'Aubigné's "au lecteur" serves to reinforce the open character of this type of devotional writing.

The fact that the openness of "au lecteur" applies only to Protestant, and not Catholic readers, however, becomes clearer in the "tu/vous" discussion. d'Aubigné begins the paragraph with a statement that apparently attempts to underplay the Protestant/Catholic controversies:

> Vous ne treuverez ici aucune piccoterie de nos controverses. A une seule difference vous cognoistrez de quelle Religion je fais profession. C'est que je parle par unité à Dieu qui est seul, ne pouvant m'accomoder à dire: *Vous estes Dieu.* (P. 494)

He then gives seemingly linguistic and literary reasons for his preference of "tu" to "vous." However, what follows this discussion goes beyond the bounds of a linguistic explanation and brings in the very controversies that were not to be mentioned. "Certes qui prendroit la loi du vulgaire, et les mignardes flateries du temps, on se lairroit en fin mener à dire en choses sacrees, *Je vous baise les mains*, comme on l'a escrit d'un prescheur Espagnol" (p. 494). The first sentence quickly transposes the reader into the realm of religious questions, beyond mere linguistic concerns; d'Aubigné makes a definite link between the two, saying that accepting the rule of the majority in one—that is, language—would lead to the same in the other—that is, sacred things. Thus, his apparent literary preference for "tu" has many more implications than he at first acknowledged.

Indeed, the mention of the Spanish preacher and his alleged *Je vous baise les mains*, which d'Aubigné presents as a quick allusion—"J'en dirois d'advantage en un discours privé"—engages the reader in a very complex intertextual dialogue about controversies between Protestants and Roman Catholics. d'Aubigné is referring to none other than his own *Confession du sieur de Sancy*, in which he makes no attempt whatsoever to hide his partisan views. The

Spaniard appears in the fifth chapter of *Sancy*, entitled *Des miseres des Huguenots*.[98] In this chapter, Sancy explains and justifies his own conversion to Catholicism. His simple argument is as follows: he has always had the same goals ("le profit, l'honneur, l'aise et la seurté") and he remained a Protestant as long as being such was compatible with his goals, but now that circumstances have changed, he has converted to Catholicism in order to remain true to his goals. The anecdote about the Spanish preacher serves as an analogy of Sancy's own dealings with the Protestants. The foreigner says "bezo los manos" to his master, which is a polite form of taking leave, signifying that one is abandoning a cause or a party,[99] and after recounting the episode of the Spaniard, Sancy proudly states: "Aussi j'en dis autant à Messieurs les Huguenots. . . ." d'Aubigné's satirical treatment of Sancy has an all too obvious target: the many self-seeking conversions to Catholicism by Protestants. More fundamentally, d'Aubigné is making the accusation that Catholicism is much more of a political, social, and professional structure than it is a true religion dealing with spiritual issues. Thus, the reference to the Spaniard makes the last paragraph of the preface much less innocuous than d'Aubigné pretends in his opening sentence. As one would expect of him, d'Aubigné is unable to avoid bringing in the many-faceted conflict that has been one of the major focuses of his entire life.[100] A simply Christian d'Aubigné, as opposed to a Protestant d'Aubigné very much hostile to Catholicism, cannot be found in any of his writings. It is not surprising that in this preface, he once again makes it clear, by a quick but very significant reference to another of his works, what his stand is and what he considers a true believer who will benefit from the *Meditations*.

As a conclusion to the preface, d'Aubigné extends an invitation to the reader: "c'est assés que par cette Epistre je convie mon Lecteur à eslever (en simplicité du langage de Canaan) ses pensees à Dieu . . ." (p. 494). All that he has talked about in the preface is summarized and finds its ultimate meaning in this invitation, for in it the discussion of language and communication with God is brought down to a personal, practical level for the reader, preparing him for a meaningful reading of the meditations, which will lead him into

---

[98] Agrippa d'Aubigné, *La Confession Catholique du sieur de Sancy*, in *Oeuvres*, ed. Henri Weber (Paris: Gallimard, 1969), pp. 641–44.

[99] Weber, notes on d'Aubigné's *Meditations*, p. 1252.

[100] Gisèle Mathieu-Castellani stresses the importance of d'Aubigné's memory of his father's words when he took young Agrippa to see the hanged conspirators of Amboise ("Mon enfant, il ne faut pas que ta tête soit épargnée après la mienne, pour venger ces chefs pleins d'honneur; si tu t'y épargnes, tu auras ma malédiction!"): "Malédiction suspendue comme l'épée de Damoclès sur la tête du fils, voué des lors à la vengence ou à la trahison" (*Agrippa d'Aubigné: Le Corps de Jézabel* [Paris: Presses Universitaires de France, 1991], p. 19).

communion with God. The key condition of the preparation involves, once again, language: one must commune with God "en simplicité du langage de Canaan." This phrase did not originate with d'Aubigné; it was an understood reference to the Protestant emphasis on Scripture and the personal appropriation of it.[101]

It was much more than a simple synonym for the Bible, however. The reference to Canaan was an extremely significant and powerful one for the Huguenots. As seen in the previous chapter, the persecuted Huguenots readily identified with the persecuted Israelites of the Old Testament, and Canaan thus became, in the words of Henri Weber, "le symbole du royaume promis aux élus."[102] In the sixteenth century, the notion of language was a key element in the definition of one's identity, and a "défence de la langue" was really an "affirmation de soi."[103] Hence, for Protestants, speaking the "langage de Canaan" was a sign of their identity as inhabitants of the Kingdom of God, his chosen people. d'Aubigné's reference to the Kingdom of God, symbolized by Canaan, undoubtedly had a deep resonance in the Protestant collective consciousness. It is one of the keys to understanding not only the dynamics of the *Meditations* themselves, but also the place of the work in the larger context of the Religious Wars and the Huguenots' struggle to impose themselves as a religious, and eventually political, force.

PROTESTANTS AND THE KINGDOM OF GOD

The notion of the Kingdom of God comes of course directly from the Bible.[104] The reformed teaching on this important topic was that Christ had inaugurated it spiritually in his first coming and would bring its fulfillment in his second coming. Calvin sums it up thus:

> Ainsi, Christ, afin de fonder notre espérance sur les cieux, prononce que son royaume n'est pas de ce monde. Bref, quand chacun de nous entend dire que le règne de Christ est spirituel . . . il se doit transporter à l'espérance d'une meilleure vie, et se tenir assuré que s'il est maintenant

---

[101] Weber, notes on d'Aubigné's *Meditations*, p. 938.

[102] Ibid., p. 938.

[103] Pierre Trescases, "La Naissance du discours linguistico-nationaliste ou le double mythe de la supériorité et de l'universalité du français," unpublished manuscript, p. 3.

[104] Hence, the theme was just as familiar to Catholics as to Protestants. Indeed, the events of the sixteenth century were the source of much reflection on God's Kingdom by both sides. What is shown in this chapter, however, is that Protestants had a unique conception of this Kingdom and their role in it; the next chapter will show how the Protestant conception of the Word fit into the establishment and working out of the Kingdom, the whole resulting in a particularly Protestant approach to the Kingdom in d'Aubigné's *Meditations*.

sous la protection de Jésus-Christ, c'est pour en recevoir le fruit entier au siècle à venir.[105]

The insistence on the "spirituality" of the Kingdom in no way implies unreality or irrevelance for the present age, but rather focuses on its eternal nature, because it operates in an unseen realm that is not attached to the temporal, material world. The Kingdom is thus both here and still to come, both now and not yet. This tension is reflected in some of the earliest Huguenot songs, such as the *Chanson pour protester de servir à Dieu toute sa vie* (1532):

> Ce Roy de gloire
> Est ma victoire
> A tout jamais l'honereray.

And then the fourth stanza:

> Ce Fils unique
> Abbat l'inique;
> Il est là sus
> Ce Roy Jesus
> Avec le Père
> Auquel j'espère:
> Les esperans n'y font deceus.[106]

These two stanzas contain a latent summary of the basic principles of the Kingdom. Christ is the one who "abbat l'inique," which refers to both the initiation of the Kingdom in his first coming, and the final triumph over all iniquity at his second coming. The Kingdom is a reality for the believer in the here and now—thus Christ is his "victoire"—but there is also a yearning for the consummation of the Kingdom in the future—"auquel j'espère."

This yearning involved much more than a passive hope in Christ's second coming. As "children of the Kingdom" who had already entered into its power in the spiritual realm, Protestants saw themselves not only as recipients of

---

[105] Jean Calvin, *L'Institution chrétienne, Livre II*, p. 250. He comments further, "Ce que nous avons dit, que la nature et utilité du règne de Jésus-Christ ne se peut autrement comprendre de nous, que quand nous le connaissons être spirituel, se vérifie assez parce que notre condition est misérable tout le cours de la vie présente, où il nous faut batailler sous la croix. Que nous profiterait-il donc d'être assemmblés sous l'empire du Roi céleste, si le fruit de cette grâce ne s'étendait plus loin que l'état de la vie terrienne? Il nous convient donc de savoir que tout ce qui nous est promis de félicité en Jésus-Christ n'est point attaché aux commodités externes, pour nous faire vivre joyeusement et en repos, nous faire fleurir en richesses, nous égayer à notre aise et sans souci, et jouir des délices que la chair a accoutumé de rechercher: mais plutôt que le tout se doit rapporter à la vie céleste."

[106] Henri-Léonard Bordier, *Le Chansonnier Huguenot du XVIe siècle* (Geneva: Slatkine Reprints, 1969), pp. 23–24.

spiritual blessings but also as active participants in the building of the Kingdom. As expressed in the *Chanson lamentable* of around 1545, it was understood that believers had a necessary but difficult role to play:

> Jesus Christ nous exhorte
> Disant: Qui veut venir
> Après moy, faut qu'il porte
> Sa croix pour m'ensuyvir
> Ainsi serons receus
> Au Royaume là sus![107]

At the same time, the difficulty and pain involved in the believer's participation in the Kingdom was counterbalanced by the triumphant reality involved.
This can be seen in the *Chanson de l'oraison dominicale* by Mathieu Malingre
(1533):

> Et ton royaume precieux
> Advienne, qui florisse en renom.
> Pere trés sainct, pere trés bon,
> Nous tes enfans
> Y aspirons de grand'randon
> Pour estre avec toy triumphans.[108]

The triumph mentioned here is not Christ's alone; rather, Christians are vic-
torious with him. The Kingdom is conceived of as Christ's victory over evil, but
it is a conquest that is realized as Christ works through the Church and provi-
dentially in the world. In this manner, individual believers share in the further
manifestation of the Kingdom and consequently later in its glory in eternity.

The Myth of the Kingdom in the *Meditations*

In *The Great Code*, Northrop Frye defines myths as

> the stories that tell a society what is important for it to know, whether
> about its gods, its history, its laws or its class structure . . . mythical
> therefore means the opposite of "not really true": it means being
> charged with a special seriousness and importance.[109]

In this sense, the story of the Kingdom of God was indeed a myth for the
Huguenots, for it gave structure and meaning to their existence. This social

---

[107] Ibid., p. 345.
[108] Ibid., pp. 20–21.
[109] Northrop Frye, *The Great Code. The Bible and Literature* (San Diego: Harcourt Brace
Jovanovich, 1982), p. 33.

aspect of myth, however, is for Frye the secondary sense of the term, the first being that of a plot or narrative structure intimately linked with literature.[110] Because a myth expresses a deep, fundamental truth for the given society, as a narrative structure it is applicable to most any particular event. Frye explains:

> Poetry expresses the universal in the event, the aspect of the event that makes it an example of the kind of thing that is always happening. In our language, the universal in the history is what is conveyed by the *mythos*, the shape of the historical narrative. A myth is designed not to describe a specific situation, but to contain it in a way that does not restrict its significance to that one situation. Its truth is inside its structure, not outside. . . .[111]

Hence, it is in the literature of the times that one would expect to find the embodiment of the Kingdom myth of the Huguenots, and, as the phrase "en simplicité de Canaan" suggests, it is precisely this myth that underlies *Les Meditations sur les Pseaumes*.

When considering the story structure of the myth of the Kingdom of God, it is necessary first to turn to the Bible, from which the myth comes. In this, Frye is once again most helpful, for after his general treatment of myth in *The Great Code*, he examines at some length the story structure of the Bible, which he believes can be reduced to a U-shaped myth (apostacy, repentance, restoration—what he calls a "divine Comedy"), the basic plot of which is that eternal life is lost in the beginning (in Eden) and regained at the end (in the book of Revelation). In between these two points, the story structure is basically repeated again and again, giving an extended U-shape to the whole biblical narrative, as illustrated in the following chart:

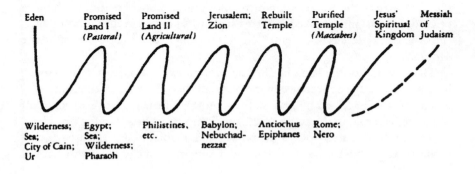

| Eden | Promised Land I (*Pastoral*) | Promised Land II (*Agricultural*) | Jerusalem; Zion | Rebuilt Temple | Purified Temple (*Maccabees*) | Jesus' Spiritual Kingdom | Messiah of Judaism |

| Wilderness; Sea; City of Cain; Ur | Egypt; Sea; Wilderness; Pharaoh | Philistines, etc. | Babylon; Nebuchadnezzar | Antiochus Epiphanes | Rome; Nero | | |

---

[110] Ibid., p. 47.
[111] Ibid., p. 46.

Frye explains:

> There is a sequence of *mythoi*, only indirectly of historical events, and
> our first step is to realize that all the high points and all the low points
> are metaphorically related to one another. That is, the garden of Eden,
> the Promised Land, Jerusalem, and Mount Zion are interchangeable
> synonyms for the home of the soul, and in Christian imagery they are
> all identical, in their "spiritual" form . . . with the kingdom of God spo-
> ken of by Jesus. . . . And the deliverers of Israel—Abraham, Moses and
> Joshua, the Judges, David, and Solomon—are all prototypes of the
> Messiah or final deliverer.[112]

This summary is basically a description of the narrative structure of the Kingdom myth itself, because it is this myth that underlies the whole Bible.

Although the actual term "Royaume des Cieux" is not found in the preface
of the *Meditations*, it appears in the individual meditations several times. For
example, more than once mention is made of Christ's words "They take by
force the Kingdom of God," referring in general to the believers' role in the
advancement of this Kingdom, and specifically to what the Huguenots perceived to be their pivotal role in the process. Also, believers are called the children of the Kingdom, which again testifies to the fact that their identity was
inextricably tied to this concept. In the same vein, the repentant individual
gains access to the "mysteries of the Kingdom," and the believer learns that
there is no comparison between this world and the Kingdom. In instances in
which the actual term is not present, the concept invades the text through a
series of synonyms and related terms. The picture of God as king and Christ
as king are found throughout. In addition, several times reference is made
to the third line of the Lord's Prayer, "Thy Kingdom come," giving evidence
to the deep desire to see God's reign established in all the world. Moreover,
the final state of the Kingdom, which will result in holy bliss for the children
of God, is constantly evoked in terms such as "la bienheureuse immortalité,"
"le Ciel," and "le siècle à venir." In this manner, the theme saturates the
Meditations.

The presence of the Kingdom in the *Meditations* is, however, not so much
linked to the actual appearance of the term. Rather, the story of the Kingdom,
exactly as it is described by Frye in his summary of the narrative structure of
the Bible, is retold in the pages of the meditations. As noted in the first chapter, one of the characteristics of the prose psalm meditations is the use of other
biblical texts within the meditations, and d'Aubigné is one of the authors, if not

[112] Ibid., p. 171.

the author, who most developed this aspect of the genre.[113] Starting from the six psalms that make up the *Meditations*, through a system of reference and allusion, he is able to bring in literally the whole story of the Bible. In the meditation on Psalm 73, he makes reference to Adam and the fall:

> Adam voulant s'accquerir la science de bien et de mal, pour se faire pareil à Dieu, trouva un Cherubin, officier du Paradis terrestre, qui le mit dehors honteusement, et puis en defendit l'entree avec un coutelas flamboyant, chastiant les outrecuidez en leurs desirs hautains. . . . (P. 528)

This statement sums up the beginning of the Kingdom story: the establishment of the original Kingdom in the garden—the "paradis terrestre"—and the original fall that is the father of all the others that come after it because they have the same root—namely, the "desirs hautains." The story, of course, does not end there, and the *Meditations* also contain numerous references to the true "ending" of the story: the consummation of the Kingdom. In the meditation on Psalm 51, for example, d'Aubigné writes: "Donne nous pour portes celles de la nouvelle Jerusalem, estoffes de gemmes et pierres precieuses" (p. 544), an obvious reference to the heavenly Kingdom. In addition, the final line of the *Meditations* ends thus: "c'est ce que nul oeil n'a peu voir, nulle oreille n'a peu ouyr, nul esprit n'a peu comprendre, et que nul coeur n'a peu desirer dignement" (p. 572), evoking the Kingdom in all of the incomprehensibility of its final and eternal stage.

In his references to other biblical texts, d'Aubigné does not limit himself to the starting and ending point of the myth. Indeed, he populates the text with a whole host of biblical personages and episodes that bring in the story of the Kingdom as it goes through the cycle of ups and downs that makes up its very structure. Various others exemplify the fall into sin and all of its consequences. Adam's own son Cain, for instance, is presented as an example not to follow: ". . . que la force des Caïns ne nous eschauffe point sur Abel" (p. 507). In addition, in the meditation on Psalm 84, sinners are compared to the Israelites going into captivity in Persia:

> On a escrit que le peuple allant en la captivité de Perse, quelques Prophetes, suivis de leurs enfans, allerent cacher les precieux meubles de l'Eglise, (et entre autres ce feu sacré, tesmoin de l'assistance de l'Eternel) dans le puits sec d'une vallée profonde . . . (P. 511),

where the act of hiding the flame signifies loss of dedication to God. At the same time, the *Meditations* are replete with references to the upward swing of the myth. David is throughout the perfect example of the repentant sinner,

---

[113] This point will be studied in greater detail in the next chapter.

and the stories of characters such as Joseph and Shadrach, Meshach and Abednego in the fiery furnace give an illustration of those who refuse to disobey God even when it means great difficulty for them. In addition, the image of the Temple runs throughout a large part of the *Meditations*, especially the one on Psalm 84, and is symbolic of restoration with God. The images of Mounts Horeb and Zion have similar functions.

In the midst of the myriad biblical personages and episodes that come to life in the pages of the *Meditations*, there is one group of related characters and events that constitutes the privileged focal point of the text: the Israelites freed from bondage in Egypt and marching to the promised land of Canaan. It is the only image that is present in all of the six meditations, and it thus runs through the whole text as a leitmotif. In the meditation on Psalm 16, the author gives a summary of the Exodus and the march into Canaan and its meaning:

> Le Dieu des armees, le grand Roi de tous les Rois, daigne bien nous prendre par la main, se faire nostre guide pour nous conduire par un petit sentier droit, mais epineux, à la porte estroite, et de là à la couronne de gloire et en son paradis. Ce fut avec grand murmure que le peuple d'Israël entra dans ce chemin. Les murmures, les eaux changees en sang, toutes les playes d'Egypte ne les pouvoyent animer à prendre ce dessein, si la main de Dieu, par le ministere de Moyse, ne les eust conduits, tirés, trainés: le labeur des pots, les tasches rengregees, le meurtre des enfants masles, et en tout le dur joug de Pharaon servit de lieu commun aux suasions de Moyse, comme les duretez de cette vie donnent commencement à l'estime de l'autre. Les deserts de quarante ans rendirent douz le nom de Canaan, et l'effroyable regard, ou souvenir de l'Egypte, corrigeoit le regret des aulx et des oignons: car c'est de la nature humaine, de vouloir toujours tourner le pied arriere: quand nous sommes dans ce sentier, qui nous conduit à vie plus heureuse, peu de Calebs et de Josuez continuent sans murmure la haine et le mespris de la vie, et servitude d'Egypte, pour aimer dignement et estimer la felicité de Canaan. (P. 569)

The story of the Kingdom is here first expressed in a sort of explanation or translation of the meaning of the story (in the first line) and then it is embodied by the story of the Exodus. The order in which this is done and the different weight given to the two elements is important, for this shows how the myth only comes to life in its expression in a concrete story. In the *Meditations*, the story of the Exodus is the master narrative for the Kingdom. Many of the episodes mentioned in the summary just quoted appear in other parts of the *Meditations*, along with a large number of other references and allusions.

The "tenebres egyptiennes," for example, are cited as an example of man's sin-fulness, as is the fashioning of the golden calf. Moses appears many times as God's deliverer, and God's assistance is symbolized by the pillar of fire and the great cloud. In all the episodes and characters that make up the event, the myth is abundantly embodied in both the downward and the upward swings. Canaan appears in these texts the symbol par excellence of the Kingdom, or the "couronne de gloire" and "paradis," as it is called here.

It is essential to note that the myth as embodied in the history of Israel in the *Meditations* is not simply an example from the past; rather, it comes alive and englobes the reader as it unfolds. At the beginning of the passage quoted in the preceding paragraph, there is a clear separation between the reader and the Israelites, for in the first sentence the author speaks of "nous," and then in the following sentence he speaks of "le peuple d'Israël." However, as the nar-rative progresses, a fusion takes place between the two. The recounting of the difficulties that the Hebrews experienced in Egypt, which made them more susceptible to respond favorably to Moses, is followed by a general statement—"comme les duretez de cette vie donnent commencement à l'estime de l'autre"—which concerns not only the Israelites but also the Huguenots, and thus serves as a sort of textual bridge spanning the historical gap between the two groups. Hence, in the next sentence the descriptions of the forty years in the desert and the longing to return to Egypt do not concern only the Israel-ites but also "nous" ("quand nous sommes dans ce sentier . . ."). In the end, the reader and the Israelites become one, for "nous" and the "Calebs et Josuéz" come together on the path leading to the Kingdom.

This assimilation of the Huguenots with the Israelites through the image of Canaan is even more explicit in the following passage from the meditation on Psalm 133:

> Encore pouvons nous marquer comment ceste liqueur passant sur l'ephod fait souvenir les douze tribus des beneficences, et entre toutes de la prise de possession de Canaan. Et la France, imitant les douze lignees, a voulu estre separee en douze Provinces soubs douze pairs, doit avoir en l'estomac, en la place de l'Ephod, la mesme obligation du passage de Payen au Christianisme qu'ont receu les Hebreux au tra-verser du Jordain. (P. 498)[114]

What is even more striking, however, is the link that d'Aubigné makes be-tween the occupation of Canaan and Christianity. In a sense he "collapses"

---

[114] This passage is indicative of d'Aubigné's tendency and ability to associate various passages, which sometimes seem unrelated, with each other. His association of the march into Canaan with the oil running down the High Priest's ephod is most original, and illustrates his preoccupation with the Kingdom of God.

the Kingdom myth and retroactively interprets it in the spiritual sense that is
fully revealed in the New Testament. In the paragraph that follows the section
above, the author gives a sort of explanation of the association he has just
made between the two: "Oserions-nous point approprier aux choses susdites
le Baptesme en la place du Jordain, où S. Jean l'exerça, et où Nostre Seigneur
le voulut recevoir . . ." (p. 498). The river Jordan provides the link between
Canaan and Christianity, for in both cases it stands for the same reality. The
Israelites' crossing over into Canaan was symbolic of their departure from
their old ways and the embracing of a new life of fellowship with God in his
Kingdom. Baptism, as instituted by Jesus, has exactly the same significance in
its spiritual form, for it signifies death to the old, sinful life and entrance into
the spiritual Kingdom. Hence, Canaan was simply a shadow of the true,
complete meaning of the Kingdom that was to be revealed and inaugurated
with the coming of Christ, and in this manner d'Aubigné is able to retain the
privileged image of Canaan as representative of the Kingdom while developing the full significance of the image.

The bold equation of the situation of France with that of the Israelites underscores the fact that the Huguenot reading of Israel's history involved
much more than finding simple similarities between the two groups. As
d'Aubigné makes clear, both peoples were bound by the "mesme obligation;"
both were taking part in the same *metanoia*, the same conversion from evil to
good. Marguerite Soulié rightly insists,

> les thèmes épiques empruntés à l'Ancien Testament ont été non seule-
> ment repris pour offrir un enseignement ou une exhortation . . . mais
> traités comme des récits historiques fraîchement vécus, présents, pour
> ainsi dire, dans l'histoire en train de se faire, propres à révéler, immédi-
> atement, son sens.[115]

Therefore it is not surprising to see that d'Aubigné so easily intermingles
himself and his fellow readers with the people of Israel in the pages of the
Meditations, for the two groups are simply different actors taking part in exactly the same story—that of the Kingdom.

In this appropriation of the Kingdom myth, one aspect of the story
of Canaan in particular is very important for the Huguenot's perception of
themselves as Israel, as seen in the following passage:

> C'est une charité hors la mesure de nos sens, que le Tout Puissant cre-
> ateur de tout l'Univers, conservateur de tout ce qui a estre, qui a pour
> haut dais les cieux des cieux, la terre pour marchepied, qui seigneurie

---

[115] Soulié, *L'Inspiration biblique*, p. 5.

par tout, qui se fait obeyr sans peine en toutes ses seigneuries, ait voulu choisir de tant de Royaumes un Royaume, de tant de Provinces Canaan, de tant de montaignes Sion, de tant de peuples un peuple acquis, sainct et separe. . . . (P. 545)

Once again, God's relationship with his children is conceived of in terms of the Kingdom, and the special emphasis here is on the exclusive nature of the establishment of this Kingdom. In other words, Canaan is for d'Aubigné significant in that it illustrates the doctrine of election. This becomes even clearer in the paragraph that follows:

Mais voici une seconde charité qui surpasse la premiere, que la nation esluë ayant renoncé ou crucifié le Sauveur et Dieu de Gloire, il a mis la main sur nous, et sans occasion de choix, en ce qui estoit du nostre, nous a tirés d'entre les idolatres courans aprés les bois et la pierre, pour nous adopter en la place et au rang des enfans d'Abraham. . . . (P. 545)[116]

As before, the subject here is "nous," and this can be understood in two different ways. First, "nous" refers to all Gentiles to whom the gospel of Christ was made available after the Jews rejected it, and the Huguenots were simply part of that larger group. In addition, however, there is a more precise meaning, referring to the Huguenot's specific situation in France. Just as the Jews had rejected the truth being revealed to them, so had the Catholics in France, and just as the Gentiles had been called to build the one true church, so had the Huguenots in France.[117]

The Huguenots' belief in their special role in advancing the Kingdom was a powerful force in fashioning their identity and guiding their conduct. The establishment of the Kingdom took place on many different levels for them. As Jean Delumeau rightly asserts, the root causes of the Reformation were spiritual, and so the Kingdom was first of all a private, internal affair for the individual.[118] As a child of God, the believer's goal was to master his own sinful nature and live for the glory of God:

C'est déjà un grand point de dire que nous sommes consacrés et dédiés à Dieu, pour ne plus rien penser dorénavant, parler, méditer ni faire,

---

[116] At the same time as he reinforces and accentuates the doctrine of election by speaking of the elect and the lack of choice on man's part, he also brings Christ into the picture and once again gives the image of Canaan its full interpretation as the Kingdom in its spiritual reality.

[117] Canaan is not specifically mentioned here, but it is nonetheless present in a spiritual sense, for the predestination spoken of here is synonymous with God's choice of the Hebrews.

[118] Jean Delumeau, *Naissance et affirmation de la Réforme* (Paris: Presses Universitaires de France, 1969), pp. 277–78.

sinon à sa gloire; car il n'est licite d'appliquer chose sacrée à usage prophane.[119]

It certainly did not end there, though, for this call to holiness was for God's people as a whole, not just for isolated individual believers. God had called the "peuple d'Israël" for a special mission; in the same way, he was calling the Huguenots as a "people" to do his will in France.

The sense of corporate identity grew stronger among the Protestant believers in France as the century progressed and manifested itself in the transition from scattered bands of "luthériens," as they were often called earlier in the century, to the Eglises Réformées de France. Although this organization was undertaken for the spiritual welfare of the believers, it had other consequences, as E. G. Léonard points out: "le protestantisme français ne pouvait pas . . . se constituer à part en Eglises nettement délimitées et fermement organisées sans prendre la figure et la mentalité d'un parti."[120] d'Aubigné himself says as much in *Sa vie à ses enfants*: "le Parti estoit attaché à la Religion."[121] This outlook is a key for a full understanding of the "passage du Payen au Christianisme" in France spoken of in the meditation on Psalm 133: it was a spiritual affair, but one that was to be lived out on the national level, with all that entailed.[122]

In this context, the phrase "en simplicité du langage de Canaan" takes on a very significant meaning. d'Aubigné's use of the same term in *Les Tragiques* is relevant at this point. In *Princes*, he writes:

> Cette langue qui prie est sallie en ordures,
> Les mains que vous joignez ce sont des mains impures:
> Dieu tout vrai n'aime point tant de feintes douleurs,
> Il veut estre flechi par pleurs, mais autres pleurs;
> Il esprouve par feu, mais veut l'ame enflammee
> D'un brasier pur et net et d'un feu sans fumee.
> Ce luth qui touche un pseaume a un mestier nouveau,
> Il ne plaist pas à Dieu, car il est macquereau;
> Ces levres qui en vain marmottent vos requestes
> Vous les avez ternis en baisers deshonnestes,
> Et ces genoux ployez, dessus des licts vilains,
> Prophanes, ont ployé parmi ceux des putains.

---

[119] Calvin, *L'Institution chrestienne, Livre III*, p. 154.

[120] Emile G. Léonard, *Histoire générale du protestantisme*, vol. 2 (Paris: Quadrige/Presses Universitaires de France, 1961), p. 94.

[121] Agrippa d'Aubigné, *Sa vie à ses enfants*, ed. Gilbert Schrenck (Paris: Nizet, 1986), p. 142.

[122] The meditation on Psalm 133 is by far the most political of d'Aubigné's meditations. It deals with the roles of all the members of the body politic.

Si depuis quelques temps vos rhymeurs hypocrites,
Desguisez, ont changé tant de phrases escrites
Aux prophanes amours, et de mesmes couleurs
Dont ils servoyent Satan, infames basteleurs,
Ils colorent encore leurs pompeuses prieres
De fleurs des vieux payens et fables mensongeres:
Ces escoliers d'erreur n'ont pas le style apris
Que l'Esprit de lumiere apprend à nos esprits,
De quell'oreille Dieu prend les phrases flatresses
Desquelles ces pipeurs flechissoyent leurs maistresses.
Corbeaux enfarinez, les colombes font choix
De vous, non à la plume, ains au son de la voix.
En vain vous deployez harangue sur harangue
Si vous ne prononcez de Canaan la langue,
En vain vous commandez et restez esbahis
Que, desobeissans, vous n'estes obeis:
Car Dieu vous fait sentir, sous vous, par plusieurs testes,
En leur rebellion, que rebelles vous estes;
Vous secouëz le joug du puissant Roy des Rois,
Vous mesprisez sa loy, on mesprise vos loix.[123]

In this passage, addressed directly to the king, there is a direct link between religion and state. The king's crimes are conceived of in terms of language ("langue sallie, lèvres ternis en baisers, pompeuses prières"), and others recognize his evil nature by the sound of his voice ("les colombes font choix . . . au son de la voix"). What exactly is his crime? Ignorance of the "langage de Canaan."[124] Incapable of speaking or comprehending it, he has plenty to say, yet no real communication with God ("en vain vous déployez harangue . . ."), and, consequently, he has no real communication with his subjects. Furthermore, the direct result of his disobedience toward God is that of his subjects toward him. Echoing the notion of a double covenant,[125] d'Aubigné presents a theological justification of the Huguenot rebellion: it is a sign from God himself that the king is the truly rebellious one. Refusing to submit to the reign of Christ and follow his law, the king finds himself justly despised and disobeyed. The troubles in the Kingdom of France are thus portrayed here in

---

[123] Agrippa d'Aubigné, *Les Tragiques*, in *Oeuvres*, ed. Henri Weber (Paris: Gallimard, 1969), p. 64.

[124] The text refers immediately to the "rhymeurs," but they are the kings "rhymeurs" writing for him, and thus they are speaking for him. Hence, what is said about them really applies to the king. That is why d'Aubigné returns to the subject "vous" at the end.

[125] See p. 122.

relationship to the Kingdom of God, for it is in refusing the preeminence and blocking the advancement of the latter that the king of the former stands condemned.

Of special significance is the definition of the "langage de Canaan" that d'Aubigné gives in this passage from *Princes*: "Ces escoliers d'erreur n'ont pas le style apris/Que l'Esprit de lumière apprend à nos esprits." According to this definition, the "langage de Canaan" is a "style," a manner of speaking. On one level this referred to the influence of biblical language on the speech of re-formed believers.[126] Its true significance, however, was not so much in any outward linguistic conventions, but rather in what these conventions signified. Pierre Bourdieu's comments on style in *Ce que parler veut dire* are useful for understanding the significance of this definition. For Bourdieu, one style in relation to others "reçoit une valeur sociale et une efficacité symbolique" and

> Parler, c'est s'approprier l'un ou l'autre des styles expressifs déjà consti-tués dans et par l'usage et objectivement marqués par leur position dans une hiérarchie des styles qui exprime dans son ordre la hiérarchie des groupes correspondants.[127]

Style is thus first a question of social distinction, and it is certainly true that the distinction between Protestants and Catholics was one of great social im-portance, an importance that grew throughout the century as the Huguenots became a more well-defined and public group. Donald Kelley goes as far as to say that "confession" in the Protestant sense of the word—that of making known one's beliefs—became a sort of "carte d'identité."[128] Indeed, for Prot-estants, public confession was an integral part of living out their faith. Calvin's treatise on the Nicodemites shows the virulence reserved for those who wanted to have a private, personal faith that would have no conse-quences in society. Speaking the "langage de Canaan" thus meant making a clear statement about which side one was on.[129]

One testimony to the fact that a difference in style was a crucial element of distinction between Catholics and Protestants comes from Henri Estienne's *Discours merveilleux de la vie, Actions & Deportemens de la royne Catherine de Medicis*. According to Estienne, Catherine had one goal: to govern alone, and she would do and say whatever was necessary to achieve that goal.

---

[126] Weber, notes on d'Aubigné's *Meditations*, p. 938.

[127] Pierre Bourdieu, *Ce que parler veut dire* (Paris: Fayard, 1982), pp. 60, 41.

[128] Kelley, *The Beginning of Ideology*, p. 96.

[129] Kelley quotes the *Traitté de devoir des princes*: "Confession is demonstrating publicly that you consent in no way to idolatry and communicating to others the same doctrine that you embrace" (Ibid., p. 96).

Consequently, she was really nothing but a chameleon saying different things to different people in order to get what she wanted. For instance, when she and the young King were being held captive by the Guises during the first war, she would say one thing publicly and another privately: "Cependant toutes fois ce ne sont que messages vers le Prince de Condé, lettres secrettes, entreprises cachées, tous propos contraires à ce qu'elle disait et escrivoit ouvertement à l'instance & en faveur du parti Catholique."[130] However, the death of the King of Navarre relieved her fears that he, as the first of the princes of the blood, might in some way usurp her power. Therefore she no longer felt a need to placate the Huguenot Party and thus turned away from them: "Vous l'avez veuë Huguenotte à l'envie du roy de Navarre: maintenant vous la verrez Catholique en depit du Prince de Condé."[131] Significantly, with this change in religion came a change of language. After Navarre's death, assured that she could

> tenir, sans contredit, le premier lieu au parti Catholique, & que d'ailleurs le Prince de Condé vient à estre le plus proche du sang & du gouvernement par consequent, craignant qu'il ne querelast ce droit, estant devenu le plus fort, soudain elle devient son ennemie: tellement que style de ses lettres & propos est tout autre qu'il n'estoit trois jours auparavant.[132]

Hence, Catherine's "religious conversion" manifested itself practically in a conversion of styles.[133]

Estienne might not have found Catherine's going back and forth between Huguenots and Catholics so despicable if she had truly believed in what she was saying at any given point; that is, if she had really subscribed to the "valeur symbolique," to return to Bourdieu's comments on style, represented by the different languages she was speaking. According to Estienne, however, such was not the case, for he insists again and again that she never preferred one religion over the other in the sense that she actually adhered to a set of beliefs. She was simply doing what was politically expedient. Perhaps Catherine de Medicis was not fully aware of the implications involved in shifting back and forth between the official language of the traditional church and state and that of the Huguenots. The implications were nonetheless vast

---

[130] Estienne, *Discours*, pp. 27–28.

[131] Ibid., p. 29.

[132] Ibid.

[133] In his *Histoire Universelle*, d'Aubigné also accuses Catherine de Medicis of trying to speak the "langage de Canaan" in order to influence Protestant representatives. *Histoire Universelle*, ed. Alphonse de Ruble, vol. 5 (Paris: Librairie Renouard, 1886–1909), p. 363.

and went far beyond any mere choice of words. It is the second element of d'Aubigné's definition of the "langage de Canaan," "Que l'Esprit de lumiere apprend à nos esprits," that reveals the distinctive character of the symbolic vision of the world linked to the "langage de Canaan." For what is immediately evident—and this is undoubtedly what d'Aubigné is referring to when he speaks of "en simplicit"—is that the "langage de Canaan" needs no hierarchical intermediary. The style spoken of in *Princes* is thus synonymous with the one described in the preface of the *Meditations*, the style of Scripture that results in strengthened communion between the true believer and God.

The "langage de Canaan" was therefore a language of "immédiateté,"[134] a language of communication between the true believer and God. Of course, as a Protestant, d'Aubigné held that, properly speaking, there is only one mediator between God and humans—Jesus Christ; and of course, the means of grace—preaching and the sacraments—are communicated among those whom d'Aubigné argues are intermingled with Israel crossing into Canaan, the promised land. Nevertheless, there is a sense in which one can speak of the "langage de Canaan" as being a language of communication between humans and God.

For the Huguenots, the challenge to the existing authorities implicit in the "langage de Canaan" was experienced not in terms of a threat but in terms of the hope of establishing the Kingdom. At the beginning of the wars, there was much enthusiasm and the hope that they were playing a unique role in ushering in the Kingdom by bringing about a temporal manifestation of it on earth, one that would be a sort of first fruits of the eternal Kingdom to come. This is reflected, for example, in the *Chanson spirituelle de l'assistance que Dieu a faite à son eglise a Lyon en 1562*, which makes the following invitation:

> Venez fidles du Christ
> Tous pour chasser l'Antechrist,
> Car Dieu pour nous a mandé
> Le bon prince de Condé.[135]

The Prince of Condé, a figure in space and time, is elevated to a participant in the eternal spiritual realm, which shows how the perceived strengths and victories of the Protestants were for them a sure sign of the advancement of the Kingdom. Even more important in this respect was the person of Henri de Navarre, who represented the real possibility of a Protestant king, and thus

---

[134] The term is from Crouzet, *Les Guerriers de Dieu*. One of his main tenants is that the major difference between Protestants and Catholics is the difference between "immédiateté" and "immanence."
[135] Bordier, *La Changonnier Huguenot*, p. 249.

a Protestant kingdom that could begin to alleviate the discordance between God's spiritual reign and the present age, moving ever closer to the establishment of the Kingdom in all its fullness.

The vicissitudes of the Religious Wars, although punctuated by moments of seeming triumph for the Huguenots, eventually cast serious doubt on this conquest of Canaan. The various massacres that took place—the most notable being of course that of Saint Bartholomew's Day—gave a sobering reminder of the Huguenots' status as a persecuted minority in France, and serious infringements of the various edicts decreed to end the individual wars often occurred. This did not, however, cause a crisis in the Huguenots' perception of themselves as God's children, for, as Marguerite Soulié has shown, in the latter half of the century the emphasis shifted from the theme of the Israelites marching victoriously into Canaan to the message of the prophets calling the Israelites to repentance.[136] In this way, the losses and the massacres that the Huguenots suffered could be interpreted as coming from God's loving hand, in that they were a call to repentance and to turning back to God in a wholehearted reliance on his strength alone to bring them to the Promised Land. In addition, in his *Du Droit des Magistrats*, Bèze makes it clear that even if God is allowing the enemy to prevail in order to discipline and cleanse his people, the fight for the true Kingdom, that is, the battle against evil, must continue:

> Je di doncques . . . qu'il ne faut point juger par le seul evenement bon ou mauvais, si une chose a esté justement ou injustement entreprise. Car (pour parler plus chrestiennement) nostre Dieu souventesfois punit tellement les fautes des hommes, ou bien esprouve les siens, que leurs conseils (encores que ils soient bons et droits d'eux-mêmes) toutesfois ne succedent selon leur intention. Ce qui se void notoirement en la guerre des Tributs d'Israël contre les Benjamites; si est-ce que pour cela Dieu ne laisse pas d'estre tousjours juste en ses faits de quelque instrument qu'il se serve, et les peuples aussi ne laissent pas d'avoir eu bon droit contre leurs ennemis, encores que par un juste jugement ils aient porté les coups.[137]

In other words, there can be no capitulation in the face of a state that would deny its members the right to the freedom of their conscience. Hence, in spite of the incredible odds against them—or perhaps because of them, because they were so reminiscent of the giants of Canaan that the Israelites came up against—the Huguenots persevered in their conquest of Canaan.

---

[136] Soulié, *L'Inspiration biblique*, p. 87.

[137] Théodore de Bèze, *Du droit des magistrats sur leurs subjets*, ed. Robert Kingdon (Geneva: Droz, 1970), pp. 12–13.

The practical manifestation of this struggle was the establishment of what became known as "l'Etat Huguenot."[138] Unwilling—indeed unable—to submit to an authority that denied them liberty of conscience, the Huguenots set up a governmental structure that allowed them to follow their consciences and live an immediate, transcendent relationship with God. One could say then that the "langage de Canaan" was the official language of the Huguenot State, because, as Bourdieu puts it, "l'unification linguistique se confond avec la construction de l'état monarchique."[139] In other words, the "langage de Canaan," as the embodiment of the ideological uniformity found among the Huguenots, was an integral aspect of the political struggles of the Religious Wars. It was, on the one hand, synonymous with the type of government the Huguenots hoped to establish, and, on the other hand, it was an impediment to the linguistic unification the official church was trying to maintain.[140]

Not surprisingly, the myth of the Kingdom figures prominently among the arguments given to justify the Huguenot rebellion and the establishment of the State within the State. Just as the reformers had turned to the history of Israel for spiritual guidance, so the "monarchomaques" consulted the same Old Testament narratives for political guidance.[141] In his *Vindiciae contre Tyrannos*, Mornay, in answering the question "S'il est loisible de resister à un Prince qui veut enfraindre la loi de Dieu ou qui ruine l'Eglise," follows the example of Bèze and turns to Israel:

> Car si tel ca a esté loisible au peuple de Juifs . . . voire mesme si cela leur a esté enjoint, je croy que lon maccordera qu'il faut en accorder autant à tout un peuple chrestien de quelque royaume & pays que ce soit.[142]

The basis of this whole argument, as in Bèze's treatise, is God's covenant with the people of Israel, symbolized by Canaan:

> En premier lieu, il faut ici considérer que Dieu ayant choisi Israel d'entre tous autres peuples, pour luy estre peuple peculier, fit alliance avec, à ce qu'il fust peuple de Dieu. Cela est escrit en plusieurs endroits du

---

[138] Cf. Léonard: "une nouvelle espèce de république composée de toutes ses parties et séparée de l'Etat, qui avait ses lois pour la religion, le gouvernement civil, la justice, la discipline militaire, la liberté de conscience, la levée des impôts, l'administration des finances" (*Histoire générale*, vol. 2, p. 130).

[139] Bourdieu, *Ce que parlar veut dire*, p. 29.

[140] Censure of books and bans on preaching were just two of the ways that the Church tried to maintain its monopoly of the linguistic market.

[141] Actually, the division between spiritual and political leaders is a false one, Bèze being the best example of the fact that the two were often one in the same.

[142] Estiene Iunius Brutus [Philippe Du Plessis-Mornay], *Vindiciae contra tyrannos* (1581), ed. H. Weber (Geneva: Droz, 1979), p. 47.

Deuteronome. La substance & teneur de ceste alliance estoit, que tous fussent soigneux en leurrs lignees, tribus & familles en la terre de Chanaan, de servir purement à Dieu, lequel voulait avoir une eglise dressee à jamais au milieu d'eux. . . . [143]

For Mornay, this covenant is also at the center of the monarchy established by God in Israel: "Or après que le Rois eurent esté donnez au peuple, ce pact au lieu d'estre rescindé fut renouvellé & confirmé pour iamais." [144] He then goes on to explain the principle of the "double alliance," by which God makes a covenant with both the king and the people, and if one fails to uphold the true church, the other is responsible before God to do what is necessary to remedy the situation. Mornay does not only state this in theoretical terms but brings it home forcefully for the Huguenots:

Mais si le Roy passe outre, & envoye des lieutenants qui nous contraignent d'estre idolatres, & s'il nous commande de chasser Dieu du milieu de nous, fermerons nous pas la porte au Roy & à ses officiers plustost que chasser hors de nostre ville le Seigneur Dieu qui est le Roy des Rois? [145]

Here he asks the Huguenot readers to consider their actions in light of the Kingdom of God, and to remain faithful to the precepts of the Kingdom at all times.

THE HUGUENOT STATE AND THE CATHOLIC STATE

The Huguenot resistance and establishment of their own special "State within the State" proved to be a very potent force in the years following the Saint Bartholomew's Day massacre. The strength of their position is reflected in the "Edit de Beaulieu" of 1576, which bestowed upon them greater rights than they had ever enjoyed before. [146] Although, of course,

---

[143] Ibid.

[144] Ibid., p. 50.

[145] Ibid., pp. 73–74.

[146] "Et pour ne laisser aucune occasion de troubles et différends entre nos sujets, avons permis et permettons l'exercise libre, public, et général de la religion prétendue réformée par toutes les villes et lieux de notre Royaume, et pays de notre obéissance et protection de temps et personnes, ni pareillement de lieux et places, pourvu qu'iceux lieux et places leur appartiennent, ou que ce soit du gré et consentement des autres propriétaires, auxquels ils pourraient appartenir. Esquelles villes et lieux ceux de ladite religion pourront faire prêches, prières, chants de psaumes, administration du baptême, et de la cène, publication et célébration de mariages, écoles et leçons publiques, correction selon ladite religion, et toutes autres choses appartenant au libre et entier exercise d'icelle. Pourront aussi tenir consistoires et synodes, tant provinciaux que généraux, appeler nos officiers ès lieux où lesdits synodes seront convoqués et assemblés: auxquels synodes généraux et provinciaux enjoignons nosdits officiers d'assister, ou aucun d'eux." The text goes on to explain that the only exceptions to these privileges are Paris and the surrounding area as well as the king's court (André Stegmann, ed., *Edits des guerres de religion* [Paris: Vrin, 1979], p. 88).

extremely advantageous to the Huguenots, such concessions to "heretics" were considered unacceptable by many Catholics and thus became the starting point of the formation of the "Sainte Ligue." For E. G. Léonard, the League constituted an "Etat catholique en face de l'Etat protestant et de l'Etat royal,"[147] and, as such, it is the standard against which to measure the Huguenot State and the "langage de Canaan." For although the Huguenots were ostensibly at war with the crown, which was officially Catholic, the king, in his attempts to gain peace (and sometimes to keep his own power), often played the two religious forces against each other. This simply underscores the fact that the real battle was between Protestants and Catholics, and the League, in the intensity of its fervor provoked by the advancement of the heretic cause, capsulized the very essence of the differences between these two opposing factions.

The history of the League is often recounted only in terms of its political maneuvering—especially those of the Guises—and with little emphasis on the spiritual nature of the group. In his work, *Les Guerriers de Dieu*, Denis Crouzet has taken pains to re-establish the spiritual context of the League.[148] For him, the League was closely related to the many strains of mysticism in Catholicism, strains that intensified after around 1575 and played a more pivotal role in the spirituality of the times than is usually acknowledged.[149] Some of the most important texts for this mysticism were meditations like the ones examined in the preceding chapter, which called for a sensorial contemplation and union with Christ. As Crouzet explains, "Le catholique zélé est un homme qui existe en Dieu, qui se sent et se sait investi sacralement."[150] In other words, the "ligueurs" of the late sixteenth century, in their mystical relationship with God, embodied the Catholic notion of immanence that the "langage de Canaan" opposed. The language of the League can thus be characterized as what Michel de Certeau calls the "langue de Dieu," which, like the "langage de Canaan," attempted to overcome the effects of Babel.[151] This was done, however, not by "respeaking" God's word into the human situation, but rather by God actually speaking though the believer. Although the "langage de Canaan" was a rational appropriation of God's Word through

---

[147] Léonard, *Histoire générale*, vol. 2, p. 131. See also, Mack P. Holt, *The French Wars of Religion, 1562–1629* (Cambridge: Cambridge University Press, 1995), esp. the prologue: "Gallicanism and Reform In the Sixteenth Century."

[148] See Denis Crouzet, *Les Guerriers de Dieu*, vol. 2 (Paris: Champ Vallan, 1990), chaps. 16–19.

[149] Ibid., pp. 440–45.

[150] Ibid., p. 427.

[151] Certeau, *La Fable Mystique*, p. 216.

Scripture, the "langue de Dieu" was a mystic invasion of the individual by God's very words.[152]

For the "ligueurs," this type of language was also closely associated with the myth of the Kingdom. The turmoil and strife of the Religious Wars were interpreted as signs of Christ's imminent return: "L'histoire que les liguers tentent de promouvoir est mystiquement anticipatrice du Règne de Dieu. Elle est la fin de l'Histoire."[153] This "règne de Dieu" they were awaiting was totally different from that of the Protestants. As Crouzet explains, there was a great "angoisse eschatologique" among Catholics near the end of the century, and their response to this was

> une extraordinaire tentative de conformation de la société temporelle à la société céleste, dans l'Union à Christ de tous, une tentative qui était inscrite dans une certaine situation d'urgence sotériologique.[154]

Thus, the anticipation of the coming of the Reign of Christ—while holding forth the possibility of eventual union with God—was also a fearful prospect and called for an attempt to attain personal piety in order to be found worthy of the coming Kingdom. Hastening the second coming of Christ through the conformity of this world to the next, and thus the establishment of Canaan through an effort of being filled by God—such was the "langue de Dieu" of the League.

The belief that the end of the world was at hand and that the Kingdom of God would come into full fruition with Christ's return was, of course, also prevalent among the Huguenots, but the different way they approached it points again to the distinctive character of the "langage de Canaan." As noted above, the continual defeats in the wars shattered hopes of an earthly "moment" of the Kingdom. Although disappointing for the Huguenots, it was not devastating, for any temporal manifestation of the Kingdom had only been considered important in relationship to the final, spiritual kingdom.

---

[152] Certeau compares the "langue de Dieu" with divine communication as Calvin speaks of it in the preface to the 1543 edition of the psalms: "Dieu nous met en la bouche les paroles comme si lui-même chantoit en nous." For Certeau, the difference between Calvin's language and the "langue de Dieu" is that the mystics tried to overcome the "comme si" (Ibid., pp. 219–20).

[153] Crouzet, *Les Guerriers*, p. 446.

[154] Ibid., p. 448. Cf. p. 407: "En la profondeur mythique de la Ligue, il y aurait l'exacerbation de l'angoisse biblique de la faute et de l'infidélité. L'ire divine significative de l'abomination du peuple et de la fin des Temps hante les hommes. L'on peut se demander alors si la lutte qui s'engagea contre le roi et ceux qui lui étaient fidèles ou s'alliaient à lui, ne fut pas l'instrument nécessaire à un dépassement de l'angoisse eschatologique, ou ne permit pas son inflexion rassurante en une situation millénariste. . . . En ce sens, la Ligue était une tentative de libération de l'angoisse, dans l'union spirituelle avec Dieu et dans le combat contre le monde et celui qui en est le roi."

Therefore, they continued to focus on the Kingdom by interpreting their experiences as signs of the last days, charged with even more grandeur as they were thought to be leading up to the "grand jour du Seigneur," where final justice would be established with the definitive coming of the Kingdom.

The Huguenot anticipation of the Kingdom was in this manner more positive than that of Catholics, for, although not ignoring the horrors of the times, they approached it with much confidence, and it is this confident outlook that one finds in d'Aubigné's *Meditations*. d'Aubigné is addressing fellow believers, and in this sense d'Aubigné's *Meditations* are also *Chrestiennes Méditations* like those of Bèze. As such, there is a decided emphasis on the upward swing of the U-shaped narrative described by Frye, which in the short version of the myth includes the work of Christ in redeeming the elect and establishing his Kingdom. d'Aubigné's text, as we saw in the analysis of the preface, is addressed to those who have been predestined by God to inherit the Kingdom, and who are thus assured of their place in the Kingdom when it is manifested in all its fullness at the end of time. It is thus not surprising that d'Aubigné focuses on the second, "positive" half of the myth, and one sees in this the true nature of the Canaan of the "langage de Canaan."

This emphasis on the upward swing of the myth is evident in what d'Aubigné invites the reader to experience in the last sentence of the preface. The verb that d'Aubigné uses at the beginning of the sentence— "eslever"—is the first indication of this emphasis, which is reinforced by what follows: "eslever ses pensees à Dieu . . . au sein duquel y a propitiation. . . ." One would be surprised, of course, not to find repentance playing a major role in the work, for it was well understood to be the point of entrance into the Kingdom,[155] and thus the starting point of the upward swing of the myth. Calvin wrote the following, making clear the relationship between sin and the Kingdom:

> Faites pénitence, car le royaume de Dieu est approché (Matt. 3:2). . . .
> En annonçant le royaume de Dieu, il les appelait à la foi. Car par le royaume de Dieu, qu'il annonçait être près, il signifiait la remission des péchés, le salut et la vie, et généralement tous les biens que nous recevons en Christ,

and

> Premièrement, par ces paroles, il déclare que c'est en sa personne que les trésors de la miséricorde de Dieu sont ouverts et déployés. Seconde-

---

[155] That is, from the human point of view. God's divine choice was of course considered previous to anything in the individual.

ment, il requiert la pénitence. Finalement, une confiance et assurance certaine des promesses de Dieu.[156]

Penitence is thus the basis of Kingdom life, for Christ is seen as offering wonderful treasures to his people, but it is not without a price, without a change in the person receiving: "il requiert la pénitence."

d'Aubigné's use of the word "propitiation" when dealing with this issue is highly significant, for it underscores the positive treatment of this whole issue. Although it certainly refers to sin, the emphasis is not really on the sin itself, but rather on the fact that forgiveness for this sin is available in God. This is exactly what one finds throughout the meditations. Although sin is an ever-present reality, there is no morbid preoccupation with the Christian's shortcomings, but rather a focus on the ever-present possibility of turning back to God and finding mercy. The God of the *Meditations* is, as Fragonard points out, "incompréhensiblement bon."[157] d'Aubigné definitely emphasizes the reconciliatory nature of God, which is in effect the motivating principle behind the upward swing of the Kingdom myth. He certainly does not ignore the judgmental, wrathful nature of God, but it is seen as a part of his "just" (and as such understandable[158]) reaction to sin. Indeed, the forgiveness that is available in Christ and overcomes God's just wrath is probably the greatest sign of his goodness. First, the ability and desire to repent is conceived of as a gift from God: "Le premier present est la contrition pour nos pechez . . ." (p. 503). In addition, God is very quick to forgive and transform those who are contrite: "Pour reprendre ce bon vouloir, nous ne saurions si tost dire, *Il faut confesser à Dieu nostre mesfait*, qu'aussitost l'Eternel n'ait osté la peine de nos peschez: et voila le desespoir changé en esperance . . ." (p. 513). Moreover, even when his children complain against him, God is always forgiving: "C'est cette amertume qui produit tant de hardiesse en ses serviteurs et que Dieu a pardonné en sa justice; mais il ne pardonnera point à l'inique triumphant . . ." (p. 525). The reality of sin thus never overwhelms the meditation to the point of blocking the movement of the narrative, because the reality of God's grace is always greater, forever moving things upward.

The *Meditations* contain a poignant and sensitive treatment of the inner battle of the believer, which includes dealing with the subtle attacks of the devil and always struggling with the tendency to interpret life from man's own viewpoint instead of God's. This is seen especially in the Meditation on Psalm 51, from which the following passage captures the intensity of this struggle:

---

[156] Calvin, *Institution, Livre II*, p. 89.
[157] Fragonard, *La Pensée religieuse*, p. 125.
[158] Ibid.

Le subtil [Satan] fait le mestier de peindre quand il veut: son pinceau m'a fait voir les beautez, douceur et un paradis de delices, qui demeurent quand il a changé de region, horreurs, amertumes et un enfer de torments. Le mesme qui avoit espié les heures inquietes de la nuict ou les oiseuses du jour, pour me meiner aux precipices, m'affronter à tous mes resveils de la nuict et toutes mes pauses du jour, un portrait effroyable, un vilain bouc, puant de paillardise, un espouvantable crocodile, qui pleure pour trahir, un loup qui a les dents sanglantes d'un aigneau domestique ou du petit chien fidele qui gardoit la maison; et puis sans portraict me fait dans son miroir voir ces mesmes choses en m'y voyant; lui aussi ne se presente plus comme un enfant, mais comme un vieux serpent. (P. 538)

The sinner is not condemned here because of his faults, but rather he is depicted as being at the mercy of something greater than himself. Interestingly enough, one of the greatest struggles with sin is the believer's own preoccupation with his wrongdoing, and he has to call on God's grace to relieve him from his own guilty conscience:

Desploye, Seigneur, cette main à me relever de mon odieuse bouë: tu vois la haine que je me porte à cause de mes peschez; c'est toi seul qui tires du seuil de l'Enfer mon esperance prosternee. Et comme les pensees que tu me donnes sont arres et avant-coureurs d'un plus grand otroi, meine mon esprit où ma foi et mes regards sont desjà volés, asçavoir au sein de ta grace, et au giron de tes douceurs. (Pp. 542–43)

God's goodness and grace are thus supremely manifested in the *Meditations* by the objective forgiveness that he grants to his children through the propitiation available in Christ, as well as by the subjective renewing of the mind that he brings about within the believer, leading him in an upward movement of communion with God.

Indeed, as expressed in the preface, this atonement comes "au sein de Dieu," an image that connotes an intimate encounter between two persons: the relationship of love established between the believer and God through Christ's atoning death. The image of the open breast in fact brings in another notion extremely important to this upward swing of the myth: adoption, which is how the New Testament describes the relationship between God and his children. Calvin is again helpful in explaining the relationship between the Kingdom and adoption:

Premièrement, que cela soit arrêté en notre coeur, que le royaume des cieux n'est pas un salaire de serviteurs, mais un héritage d'enfants, dont jouiront seulement ceux que Dieu a adoptés pour ses enfants (Eph. 1:5, 18): et ils n'en jouiront pour autre cause que pour cette adoption. . . . [159]

and

Si donc on demande la cause première par laquelle l'entrée nous est ouverte au royaume de Dieu, et avons le moyen d'y persévérer, la réponse est prête: c'est parce que le Seigneur nous a une fois pour toutes adoptés par sa miséricorde, et nous conserve toujours. [160]

The term adoption here is, in many ways, synonymous with predestination, in that it refers to God's sovereign choice in the adoption of his children and the assurance of his presence and care in their lives.

Accordingly, the God of the *Meditations* is portrayed as a passionate, caring Father. His care is symbolized by the image of his hand, which is present throughout the text. It is his hand that brings forgiveness: "je me presente nettoyé de ta main" (p. 542), and ushers the believer into the Kingdom: "veuilles estre par pitié mon advocat qui nous prens par la main comme enfans de la maison, nous arrachant du poing de ta justice . . ." (pp. 537–38). It also brings about great transformations:

de la mesme main qui m'a tiré du parc au palais, qui de berger m'a fait Roi, qui m'a eslevé de la bouë pour me colloquer aux honneurs, qui de la conduite des brebis m'a promeu à celle des peuples, voire d'Israël, de cette main tu me fais prescheur et pescheur d'hommes. Mutation plus miraculeuse que la premiere. . . . (P. 541)

In addition, God's hand guides the believer down the straight and narrow path:

les voluptez, ombres, frescheurs et delices que nous cerchons en nous amusant, au lieu de marcher à nostre vocation, nous sont ostez de la main du Pere, qui envoye et suscite nos envieux comme vilains et infames vers, pour piquer le kikajon, et faire mourir les verdures delicieuses, par là nous oster des mains et de la frequentation des meshants, ses ennemis, et nous chasser droit au tabernacle de Sion. (P. 515)

It is only through God's care and guidance, manifested by the works of his hand, that the believer is able to persevere until the coming of the Kingdom:

Le Dieu des armies . . . daigne bien nous prendre par la main, se faire nostre guide pour nous conduire par un petit sentier droit, mais epineux, à la porte estroite, et de là à la couronne de gloire et en son paradis. (P. 569)

---

[159] Calvin, *Institution, Livre III*, pp. 288–89.
[160] Ibid., p. 275.

God's fatherly attentiveness is also summarized in the following way in the preface: "qui se tient volontiers prés des coeurs desolez, qui n'oublie jamais la clameur de ceux qui le supplient. . . ." The image is that of a tender, compassionate parent who is lovingly involved in his children's lives. The attentiveness and care are willful—"volontiers"—and constant—"n'oublie jamais." These phrases speak to the present character of the Kingdom of God in its incomplete manifestation in this age. Although the believers are already "in" the Kingdom, there is still much pain and sorrow in this life, and because of their relationship with God, they can cry out to him in an abandoned expression of their despair and dismay, being assured that he hears their cries. Hence, in the various meditations the exercitant often calls for God's attentiveness:

> abaisse ton oreille, qui est en si haut lieu, pour recevoir ma supplication venant des lieux profonds, et du fond de mes ameres pensees: abaisse-toi, ou avance ta dextre; car mon affliction, qui est si forte pour m'accabler, est trop faible pour (sans ton secours) monter jusqu'au throsne de ta majesté. (P. 550)

With the assurance of God's care and attention, the Christian feels free to express the innermost workings of his soul:

> Tu nous a deffendu contre les fleches du jour, et les espouvanteaux de la nuict. C'est ce qui me donne la hardiesse et l'adresse à toi, pour crier jour et nuict, lors que le jour a prolongé mes destresses. . . ." (P. 549)

Indeed, the meditator does not try to cover up his emotions and pain, but rather brings them all before God, confident in his love and salvation: "Je demeure extatique en mes angoisses, les genoux à terre, mes souspirs en l'air, mes yeux au Ciel, mon coeur à toi; releve-le, Seigneur, en l'esperance de ton salut" (p. 556).

The expression of the pain and sorrow of life is actually directly related to what will come when the Kingdom is fully manifested in the age to come, which is what d'Aubigné speaks of in the last phrases of the preface: "qui ne souffre point justice estre foulee, et en qui seul aux temps calamiteux se trouvent conseil et consolation." The reference is of course to the present in that the injustice is here and now, and the consolation is needed here and now. However, the assurance of justice is based on the future realities of the Kingdom, and the ultimate counsel and consolation come from understanding how what is going on fits into God's eternal plans and from being assured that God will, in the future, bring about final and complete justice for his chosen people. Calvin explains this in the chapter of the *Institution* entitled *Meditatio futurae vitae*:

Au contraire, s'ils ont une fois élevé leurs pensées par dessus les choses terrestres, quand ils verront les iniques fleurir en richesses et honneurs, être en bon repos, avoir toutes choses à souhait, vivre en délices et pompes; voire même quand ils seront traités par eux inhumainement, quand ils endureront l'opprobre, quand il seront pillés ou affligés de quelque manière que ce soit: encore leur sera-t-il possible de se réconforter en tels maux. Car ils auront toujours devant les yeux ce jour dernier, auquel ils sauront que le Seigneur doit recueillir ses fidèles dans le repos de son Royaume, torcher les larmes de leurs yeux, les couronner de gloire, les vêtir de liesse, les rassasier de la douceur infinie de ses délices, les exalter en sa hautesse, en somme, les faire participants de sa félicité (Es. 25:8; Apoc. 7:17); au contraire, jeter en extrême ignominie les iniques qui se seront magnifiés en cette terre, changer leurs délices en horribles torments, leurs ris et joie en pleurs et grincements de dents, inquiéter leur repos par d'affreux troubles de conscience: en somme, les plonger dans le feu éternel, et les mettre en la sujétion des fidèles, qu'ils auront maltraités iniquement. Car telle est la justice, comme en témoigne S. Paul, de donner repos aux misérables et injustement affligés, et rendre affliction aux méchants qui affligent les bons, en cette journée-là où le Seigneur Jésus sera révélé du ciel (II Thess. 1:6–7).[161]

Calvin's comments illustrate Frye's assertion that the truth is inside the structure of the myth and not outside of it, for it is in the light of the upward swing itself, which stands for the establishment of the Kingdom, that everything must be interpreted. In other words, the essence of the Kingdom myth in the *Meditations* is the movement toward eternity; no point along the continuum leading to the full manifestation of the Kingdom is considered important as a static point in itself, but rather derives its significance from its relationship to what comes in the end.

The truth that is found in this structure is much more than an interpretative framework; it is the power of the Kingdom itself manifested in the present age. Calvin's summary of the *meditatio futurae vitae* is helpful for understanding this:

Pour conclure en un mot, je dis que la croix de Christ alors finalement triomphe dans le coeur des fidèles à l'encontre du diable, de la chair, du péché, de la mort et des iniques, s'ils tournent pareillement les yeux à regarder la puissance de sa résurrection.[162]

---

[161] Ibid., pp. 184–85.
[162] Ibid., p. 185.

The meditation of these things is not a passive reflection but rather an active participation in the realities of the Kingdom (here represented by the cross of Christ) that manifest themselves in the believer's life ("le coeur des fidèles"). Although in a historical sense the believer is somewhere between the second and third points of the "divine comedy," that is, between Christ's first and second coming, in a spiritual sense he experiences the reality of the complete story, for by meditating on the Kingdom myth, he experiences the power of the risen and reigning Christ.

Hence, from one end of the text to the next, everything is viewed in light of the final phase of the Kingdom. The wonderful peace celebrated in the meditation on Psalm 133 is considered important only in so far as it is an "arrhe de l'amour du Ciel, gage de cet estat parfaict, et du souverain Bien qui nous est promis en la bienheureuse immortalit" (p. 496). In addition, all the different pains, sorrows, and persecutions mentioned in the texts are eventually interpreted in light of the "jour dernier." The *Meditations* anticipate the judgment of the wicked that will take place on that day; the meditator is able to endure the evil of the present age by resting in the assurance of Christ's eventual triumph over all evil in the future. All that will come with the full fruition of the Kingdom, including judgment of evil and complete joy and happiness for the believer, invades the work and acts as a magnet pulling things upward. The believer yearns and thirsts for the Temple of God, and through this thirsting for and meditation on the future "en simplicité du langage de Canaan," the spiritual power of the Kingdom is experienced, which in turn hastens the completion of this Kingdom.

III

Speaking the "Langage de Canaan"

Les Meditations sur les Pseaumes are a concrete example of the "langage de Canaan" that was intimately linked with Huguenot identity, for in them the key concept of "en simplicité de langage de Canaan" introduced in the preface of the text is put into practice. The way Scripture is handled in the *Meditations* thus constitutes a descriptive definition of the "langage de Canaan," showing both the mechanics of its enunciation and its function in the world of the speaker. The present chapter examines both the way the "langage de Canaan" is "spoken" in and through the *Meditations* and the relationship of that language to the context in which it operates.[163]

SEEING AND SAYING

By highlighting the Kingdom myth that, according to d'Aubigné, constitutes the fundamental structure of the whole Bible, the *Meditations* fulfill the role of what Antoine Compagnon calls the "discours théologal."

---

[163] The "langage de Canaan" has not been the object of in-depth study, although it is often mentioned in passing, as in the following passage in which Madeleine Lazard describes the language of *Les Tragiques*: "qu'il combine plusieurs textes bibliques ou qu'il les reproduise avec rigueur, d'Aubigné a si intimement assimilé la langue de la Bible que *Les Tragiques* ne donnent jamais l'impression de la pasticher. La connaissance de l'hébreu, le contact permanent avec le texte, lui permettent de le transposer très fidèlement, mieux parfois que la Vulgate, mais aussi d'y faire une variété d'emprunts, références historiques, images, constructions syntaxiques (tel le génitif hébraïque: flambeau d'éternité, etc.). Il parvient ainsi à constituer une sorte de langage sacré, la 'langue de Canaan' violente et inspirée, surtout lorsqu'il s'identifie aux prophètes pour exalter, implorer Dieu, ou appeler sa vengeance" (*Agrippa d'Aubigné* [Paris: Fayard, 1998], p. 363). Barbara B. Diefendorf, without referring specifically to the term "langage de Cannaan," does define certain aspects of the language in "The Huguenot Psalter and the Faith of the French Protestants." She speaks of those who "consciously paraphrased them [the psalms] and unconsciously forged a language saturated with their rhythms, images, and metaphors" (p. 42).

> Chaque phrase de la Bible n'a de sens que par rapport à l'ensemble de la
> Bible, ou plus exactement, par rapport au réseau structuré de signifiants
> dont le graphe est exhumé de l'Ecriture par le discours théologal. . . . Et
> le discours théologal dégage cette structure, articule entre eux les signi-
> fiants dans ce réseau qui révèle justement comment chaque phrase est
> inscrite dans la structure. . . .[164]

In other words, d'Aubigné takes the individual psalms and, by emphasizing
the major themes of the Kingdom found in them, shows how they fit into the
overall framework of Scripture. This is done in the *Meditations* not through a
didactic demonstration by a learned author, but rather through a reenactment
of Scripture as the meditator assumes the role of a child of Israel. Giving this
role its full spiritual significance by relating it to Christ and the spiritual
Canaan, d'Aubigné develops the Psalms in a way that, as seen in the preceding chapter, basically retells the Kingdom story, focusing on the upward
swing of the myth. This reenactment does not take place through a discussion
about the psalms or through a comparison of the meditator's life with that of
the psalmist;[165] rather, it is realized on the level of the biblical text itself—that
is, on the level of the "langage de Canaan"—as the meditation goes from one
verse of the Psalm to the next, incorporating verses from elsewhere at various
points as it proceeds. As Compagnon explains: "le discours théologal ne peut
prétendre dégager la structure du texte qu'en la mettant en oeuvre et en la
représentant à l'image de la Bible."[166] That is exactly what d'Aubigné does in
the *Meditations*: he appropriates the "langage de Canaan;" that is, he incorporates it into his own narrative context, reactualizing each verse of the psalm—

---

[164] Antoine Compagnon, *La Seconde Main, ou le travail de la citation* (Paris: Seuil, 1979), p.
206. For Compagnon, the term applies especially to the writings of the Church Fathers, Thomas
Aquinas's work being the ultimate embodiment of this "discours": "Le monument, le modèle et
l'achèvement de la construction qui organise sans bavure tous les signifiants hérités de l'Ecriture
et de la tradition, c'est bien sûr la *Somme théologique*, et l'ensemble hiérarchisé de ses *quaestiones*
représente l'arrangement final de tous les signifiants auxquels le discours théologal eut affaire:
Dieu, la Trinité, la création, les anges, l'homme . . ." (p. 205). Although d'Aubigné's *Meditations*
are of a totally different nature than the patristic works that Compagnon refers to, they nonetheless deal with the major "signifiants" of the Bible and show how they fit together with respect to
the Kingdom myth.

[165] One does find such comparisons elsewhere in d'Aubigné's writings, as in the following
passage from the *Du debvoir mutuel des roys et des subjects*: "Comme David, nous avons fui aux
Royaumes estrangers et mesmes outre les mers: comme luy, nous avons caché nos vies dans les
cavernes et forests, et là presenté nos coeurs et nos requestes à Dieu pour luy, et puis pour nous.
Si comme luy, nous avons muni d'armes nostre innocence, comme luy, nous les avons mises bas
autant de fois que le Prince a fait semblant de poser son courroux . . ." (Agrippa d'Aubigné, *Du
debvoir mutuel des roys et des subjects*, in *Oeuvres*, ed. Henri Weber [Paris: Gallimard, 1969],
p. 472).

[166] Compagnon, *La Seconde Main*, p. 206.

"la mettant en oeuvre"—in a way that inscribes the whole meditative experience within the overall structure of the Bible—"la représentant à l'image de la Bible."

Before considering the various ways the appropriation of the biblical text within the economy of the meditations is realized, it is helpful first to examine the principles that underlie this appropriation. The apprehension of Scripture in the *Meditations* is clearly ordered around the notions of sin and repentance. This is not surprising because, as the analysis of the Kingdom myth showed above, repentance is always a crucial moment. It represents the starting point of enjoying the benefits of the Kingdom for each individual believer. When the sinner repents and asks for forgiveness, the efficacy of Christ's death begins to be realized by him or her; the sinner realizes his or her place in the Kingdom as a child of God. Repentance also represents the continual reconciliation with God that comes about as, on a daily basis after conversion, the believer deals with manifestations of his or her enduring sinful nature. In d'Aubigné's meditations, this struggle with sin is poignantly depicted as the influence and power of Satan that has to be countered and overcome by the power of Scripture in the areas of seeing and saying. A close look at this struggle reveals the way the meditations seek to take hold of Scripture so as to lead the meditator to true repentance and consequently to an experience of the power and blessings of the Kingdom of God.

The Devil of the *Meditations* is depicted as a most sinister being, whose goal is always to lead the believer away from God and down the path of destruction. He is most effective at doing this because of his ability to deceive, and Christians are constantly at risk of being fooled by Satan's mesmerizing and deleterious influence. His power is first of all exerted in the realm of what is said. In the meditation on Psalm 73, d'Aubigné describes Satan's actions in the following way:

> Enfin il a fallu esclater plus avant: car Satan, qui ne perd aucune occasion de nuire, nous dicte de plus furieuses leçons, et apprend ces textes à l'affligé: *Perisse le jour auquel je nasquis.* . . . (P. 526)

In the meditation on Psalm 16 the devil himself questions the believer's standing before God: "Qui es-tu (dit le meschant) que Dieu soit tenu à ta conservation, lui qui est si grand et si haut? Et puis quelles sont tes oeuvres?" (p. 559). In addition to these verbal assaults, the Evil One is very active in the realm of what is seen, that is, in the imagination of the believer. The meditation on Psalm 51 shows that Satan incites the individual to sin by making iniquity appear to be a beautiful thing: "L'ingenieux Daemon . . . m'ayant desguisé le nom de mon forfaict, l'adultere en amour, l'homicide en hardi, et le traistre en habile . . ." (p. 538). Moreover, after leading a person into sin, Satan later tortures him with the memories of what he has done.[166] The author sums it up thus: "desloyal peintre, qui a nos esprits pour papier, et pour tablettes nos coeurs" (p. 538). Man is obviously at the mercy of Satan, who, through his pervasive and all-encompassing power, manipulates the believer in what is said and seen.

The influence and actions of the Devil in the world are often wrought through his followers, who also accomplish their evil deeds in the realms of saying and seeing in the *Meditations*. The description that sums up all of their iniquity is that of "liar," for they speak the "vain et menteur vocable de la liberté" (p. 564). Totally deceived by Satan, they think they have found freedom, but in reality they are incapable of perceiving the truth. This leads them to the proclamation of lies and the persecution of the just, as described in the meditation on Psalm 84:

> Israel est affligé par les Balaams accueillis pour le maudire, par les Jasons, les Alcimes: car les bouches qui mesmes avoyent esté sacrees à la verité, partisans du Prince du monde, meurtriers et menteurs, accusent le peuple de Dieu, tesmoignent contre lui, trahissent Jerusalem, employent leur eloquence mercenaire à chanter le meurtre pour victoire, à avilir le sang racheté par celui de Jesus Christ, vanter les bras roides des tueurs, conter pour fange les morts de Judas, eslever la justice des Nicanors, opprimer de blasme les esgorgez, faire fleurir les uns en leur bouche et escrits par loüanges feintes et mensongeres, et vomir sur les affligés le jargon de Semei contre David fugitif, et ainsi se rendans bourreaux de leurs compagnons. . . . (P. 511)

Here the persecution of Israel—that is, the Huguenots—is described uniquely in terms of written and spoken discourse and its effects on appearances. The persecutors are able to manipulate the truth through what they say in order to make things seem other than they really are; their discourse has a semblance of beauty—"eloquence" and "louanges"—but actually it is selfish

---

[167] "Le subtil fait le mestier de peindre quand il veut: son pinceau m'a fait voir les beautez, douceur et un paradis de delices, qui demeurent quand il a changé de region, horreurs, amertumes et un enfer de torments. Le mesme qui avoit espié les heures inquietes de la nuict ou les oiseuses du jour, pour me meiner aux precipices, m'affronter à tous mes resveils de la nuict et toutes mes pauses du jour, un portrait effroyable, un vilain bouc, puant de paillardise, un espouvantable crocodile, qui pleure pour trahir, un loup qui a les dents sanglantes d'un aigneau domestique ou du petit chien fidele qui gardoit la maison; et puis sans portraict me fait dans son miroir voir ces mesmes choses en m'y voyant; lui aussi ne se presente comme un enfant, mais comme un vieux serpent.

"Ainsi les yeux qui m'attirent m'effrayent, et qui furent organes de pechés sont devenus instruments de punition" (p. 538).

and empty—"mercenaires" and "feintes." Its effects, however, are not empty, for what the ungodly so loudly and violently proclaim may be false, but it has the power to destroy, and the final fruit of their lips is death.

The story of the *Meditations* is not, however, the story of Satan's triumph over mankind, and the believer is not on his own in the battle with Satan. Because the activity of Satan is described in the realms of seeing and saying, the solution to the problem is cast in the same terms. In the same meditation in which d'Aubigné describes the subtle powers of Satan, he asks of God, "Fai-moi ouyr la nouvelle de ma delivrance par le tesmoignage intérieur de ton Esprit, qui me prononce ma grace . . ." (p. 540), and then:

> Oste de moi ce sang qui m'estonne, et me rend un spectre à moi mesme. Ouvre mes levres fermees de mon spasme, desserre mes dents que je sens grincer d'effroi, et lors ma bouche esclatera le chant de tes bontés et lors *je declarerai ton nom à mes frères, et je te louerai au milieu de la congregation.* . . . (P. 541)

d'Aubigné's requests show that God is able to counter at every point the influence of Satan and to restore the individual to a right relationship with himself. In response to Satan's accusations, which have imprisoned the individual, the voice of the Spirit *pronounces*—obviously referring to the Bible— liberating grace. The ravages of sin, here represented by blood on the hands—which stands for both the consequences of the sinner's actions for himself and others and the torturous memories (conscience) that he suffers from—are such that they prevent the meditator from perceiving reality correctly. Only God can remove the effects of the sin and allow the believer to see things the way they really are, from God's own perspective. Finally, the effects of this grace are enough to combat Satan's influence in the realm of what is said, for the blasphemous words dictated by Satan, and then the inability to speak resulting from fear, are replaced by praise for God. The content of the meditator's declaration of praise, which is a direct quote of Psalm 22, is a reminder that all of this is done through the "langage de Canaan."

The *Meditations* thus enter into this world of falsehood and misrepresentation, and, through the reactualization of Scripture they bring about, they are meant to be an answer to the lies that the believer encounters both within, in the form of Satan's questioning and images, and without, in the form of persecution by the ungodly. In the final section of the preface, the meditator was invited to experience the life of the Kingdom through the "langage de Canaan," and now in the meditations it becomes clear exactly how that is to be done. The *Occasion et argument* of the meditation on Psalm 51 makes it clear:

> Sur une repentance que fit le Roi . . . l'autheur lui fit present de cette meditation, laquelle fut . . . plusieurs fois prononcee par sa Majesté avec toutes les contenances d'un coeur contrit et repentant. (P. 536)

The meditation is meant to be "prononcée," and this obviously is not to be a mere repetition of the words on the page, but rather a reading done in the true spirit of the text. The efficacy of this act results from the fact that the meditation itself is in the "langage de Canaan," because it is a personal appropriation of the text of the Bible.

Indeed, in the *Meditations* the act of "meditating" is defined as "saying" or re-pronouncing the Bible. The preponderance of the verb "dire" is striking, and it is used for the most part as an introduction to biblical quotations or paraphrases, as in the following examples: "Aussi disons-nous avec David . . ." (p. 516), "nous confessons volontiers ce que dit le Prophete . . ." (p. 560), and "Nous pouvons dire avec Jérémie . . ." (p. 543).[168] As Fragonard says:

> Quel que soit le temps fictionnel où ces phrases sont prononcées dans notre *Méditation*, elles ont toujours été dites (écrites) antérieurement. d'Aubigné, ou la Parole Antérieure, d'avant le temps et d'avant les énonciateurs.[169]

d'Aubigné's *Meditations*, although written texts, are essentially conceived of as a reenunciation of Scripture, and, moreover, it is precisely this reenunciation of the "langage de Canaan" that brings about ultimate victory over sin as embodied in the "mauvaises langues" of Satan and his followers. This is clearly seen in the contrast that is made between the wicked and the just at the point of death. d'Aubigné describes the scene: "Dirai-je, qu'au point de la mort, en laquelle ils hurlent, nous apprenons à psalmodier à nostre Dieu, et jetter des cris d'allegresse au lieu de leurs grincements de dents" (p. 565). At this point the wicked have been reduced to no speech at all—a sure sign of their emptiness—while the children of God "psalmodient." The original meaning of the verb is "to sing," but its use here underscores the fact that it is through the "langage de Canaan" that the elect communicate with God and overcome evil.

---

[168] The verb appears approximately fifty times as an introduction to a biblical quotation. The next most frequent verb used in this context is "s'escrier" (seven occurrences), and other verbs used are "demander," "dicter," "adjouster," "crier," "confeser," "souspirer," " pronocer," "chanter," and "psalmodier." At other times there are introductions like, "C'est ce qui est marqué par ces termes: . . ." (p. 513), or "pour finir comme lui au Psaume present . . ." (p. 520). For the most part, however, the verses (or parts thereof) appear without an introduction, either as a complete sentence on their own, or as part of one of d'Aubigné's sentences.

[169] Marie-Madelaine Fragonard, "La Méditation sur les Psaumes: Monologue ou dialogue," in *La Méditation en prose à la Renaissance*, Cahiers V. L. Saulnier, no. 7 (Paris: Presses de l'Ecole Normale Supérieure, 1990), p. 97.

In addition to repairing Satan's damage in the realm of saying, one of the major tasks of the *Meditations* is to correct the wrong images that Satan plants in the believer's mind and through the light of Scripture to replace them with images that correspond to the reality of the world as God views it.[170] As Mario Richter explains, the psalms, the poetic nature of which consists mainly of imagery, provide a unique opportunity for doing just that:

> Ces images exigent le plus grand respect, la plus grande fidélité: elles sont en effet l'élément le plus précieux de la création divine; elles sont, pour ainsi dire, quelque chose qui ressemble à l'incarnation même de Dieu, la pensée divine devenue chose concrète, terrestre, visible. Les images des Psaumes pouvaient donc être considérées, d'un point de vue calviniste, comme un témoignage unique, au milieu des ténèbres du monde et de l'homme, de la condition première, originelle de la félicité d'avant la chute, quelque chose comme la préfiguration du Christ. . . .[171]

The psalmic images are divinely ordained to reveal God's thoughts in a way accessible to man. In his appropriation of these images, d'Aubigné is highly conscious of that, for he speaks of God in terms of a painter. Commenting on the two main images of Psalm 133—the high priest and the mountain—he says: "ayant esté exprimé par deux tableaux quelles sont les benedictions celestes sur les benits . . ." (p. 504), and again, in the meditation on Psalm 84: "C'est pourquoi l'Esprit despeint les deux proprietés de ce Soleil et de ce bouclier sous gloire et grace . . ." (p. 519). God is thus a true artist, one who represents things as they really are, as opposed to Satan, whose artistry is full of deception and falsehood. The difference between their productions is evident in the effect that they have on the one seeing, for although Satan's confuse and imprison, God's illuminate and liberate. Accordingly, God is constantly invoked in the *Meditations* as the giver of light and the one who disperses darkness.[172]

---

[170] The darkness Satan moves in is not one in which absolutely nothing is seen or perceived, but in which things are seen incorrectly. The meditation on Psalm 133 speaks of the link between seeing and saying: "Arriere les fables de nostre verité; il ne faut plus cercher d'ombres, puis que nous recevons du Pere de lumiere le thresor de claret . . ." (p. 496). Here the stories of man—that is, what he recounts—are contrasted with what God says—that is, the psalm being treated—and both are the expression of something else: light or darkness, truth or falsehood. Both are language—the use of words to tell a coherent story—but only one names things as they really are and allows man to perceive the world aright.

[171] Richter, "A propos des 'Chrestiennes Méditation,'" p. 65.

[172] "Je sçai que mes pechés ont fait un gros et louche nuage entre toi et moi: perce et dissipe, Seigneur, par les rayons de ton soleil de grace cet amas vicieux . . ." (p. 550). Along with numerous direct references to light: "Pere de lumieres," "ravissantes lumieres," and "lumiere inaccessible," d'Aubigné develops the common themes of God as sun or as fire, as in the following example:

The use of the images in the meditations is not restricted to those from the psalms. d'Aubigné incorporates images from the whole Bible. In the meditation on Psalm 84, for example, he writes:

> mais voulez-vous voir dans le profond du peril mortel un portraict notable de ce que peut faire ce grand *Soleil de Justice* . . . voyez flamboyer cette grande fournaise ardente de Nebucadnetsar, et le grand Ange du Ciel, qui la vient rendre plus splendide qu'elle n'estoit, y porte le bouclier d'enhaut, la rend seure aux condamnés, et pernicieuse à leurs bourreaux. . . . (P. 519)

The image of the "fournaise ardente" is not static, but rather it recalls the whole narrative of Shadrach, Meshach, and Abednego's salvation from the fiery furnace. This process occurs throughout the *Meditations* as various characters and episodes from both the Old and the New Testaments are evoked in a similar manner. Significantly, they are evoked not in a chronological fashion but rather exist side by side in a certain simultaneity that makes of them fellow participants with the meditator in the struggle between good and evil leading toward eternity.[173] In this manner, these images have an effect similar to that of the "tableaux celestes" in the "Chambre dorée" of *Les Tragiques*, about which Frank Lestringant says:

> La "lecture" des guerres de religion par les martyrs et les anges va donc s'effectuer sur le mode de la contemplation visuelle. Le passage de la chronique à une juxtaposition d'*ekphrasis* particulières trouve sa justification dans l'efficacité rhétorique de l'image: les figures actives (*imagines agentes*), directement appréhendées dans une posture dramatique, touchent davantage les sens du spectateur qu'une chronologie explicative.[174]

Although there is no formal framing of the scenes in the *Meditations*, except for the use of the terms "portraict" and "tableau," they do, nonetheless, appear within the text as a series not of flashbacks, which would place them

---

"C'est de là, o Tout Puissant, d'où la splendeur de ton conseil de feu m'as visité en mes prisons tenebreuses; c'est de là qu'a coulé le bausme celeste dans mes playes. C'est de ton saint mont que j'ay ouï la sentence de ma gloire et de ma grace, quand les meschans ont prononcé celle d'opprobre et de mort . . ." (p. 520)

For a more detailed analysis of these images in the *Meditations*, see Fragonard's *La Pensée religieuse*, vol. 2, pp. 873–905.

[173] One of the most striking examples of this is found in the meditation on Psalm 84: "il n'y a que la divinité qui se maintiene exempte des vicissitudes et decadences, tesmoin les cheutes, fautes et imperfections de tous ceux où les graces de Dieu ont abondé, depuis le parfait Adam à passer par Noë, les Patriarches, Moyse, David bien aimé, Salomon le sage, les Prophetes, Apostres, et grands serviteurs de Dieu" (pp. 517–18).

[174] Frank Lestringant, *Agrippa d'Aubigné. Les Tragiques* (Paris: PUF, 1986), pp. 78–79.

totally in the past, but rather as simultaneous occurrences. In this way they are a part of the continuous working out of the establishment of the Kingdom, and the meditator can interpret what is going on in the present through them. Hence, evoking the whole life of a character, whose own spiritual journey serves as an *exemplum*, or evoking various "high" and "low" points in the lives of biblical characters, the narrative is able to grip the reader and either comfort, console, or instruct. All of these things serve to fill the meditator's mind vividly with a correct interpretation of what is happening in his world by allowing him to see it in terms of the lives of biblical heroes. This places it within the context of the age-old struggle between good and evil, bringing encouragement and instruction that, together with the enunciation of truth the *Meditations* achieve, contribute to the eventual triumph of good.

REPORTED SPEECH AND REPORTING CONTEXT

The appropriation of the "langage de Canaan" in the *Meditations* is thus conceived of as conquering Satan's influence in the realms of seeing and saying. This takes place through an interaction between two main voices: the author–meditator's and God's.[174] It is not that the voice of Satan and his followers are silent, but they are subsumed in the voice of the author–meditator for two reasons. First, the meditator is a sinful man, and although Satan's influence on him is often represented as that of an outside force, responding to it and expressing it is still in man's nature and thus in a way his own voice. On the other hand, and this seems almost contradictory to the point just made, Satan's voice is a conquered one, because the *Meditations* are dealing with the lives of Christians. That is to say that although Lucifer is still very active and exerts a considerable amount of reckless influence, it is never an absolute power and is, at any time, susceptible to being overcome by the seeing and saying of God, when the believer appropriates them correctly. Hence, Satan's voice is not one of the major ones, and the *Meditations* focus on the Christian as he struggles to appropriate God's Word into his life.

---

[175] The designation "author–meditator" takes into account the dual nature of this first voice. The act of meditating takes place on two levels in the *Meditations*. First, d'Aubigné's composition of the texts is in itself an act of meditation. Second, the adoption of the "je" of the text in reading is also a meditation, and d'Aubigné as author is also the first one to assume this identification. This is most clearly seen in the *Occasion* for the meditation on Psalm 88, where d'Aubigné is both the author of the meditation and the one for whom it was composed. Hence, the following analysis will not separate the role of author and that of meditator, but rather focus on both in order to capture the complexity of the *Meditations*. For certain points dealing more with the author's role, the term "author" is used, and, likewise, when the analysis focuses on aspects that apply to the "je" in general, the term "meditator" is used. The term "voice" is used in a very broad sense, referring not only to written discourse but also to the author's work of selection, presentation, etc.

The retention of the first person in these texts is, of course, the first sign of the lyric aspect of the work. There is a fundamental difference between the "je" of the original psalm and the "je" of each meditation. For the original psalmist, there was no prior, authoritative word upon which he constructed his text. Rather, each word was "his," in the sense that he was the first to enunciate it.[176] The author of the *Meditations*, however, because he expresses himself and his own world through another word, must enter into dialogue with the original text and bring it into the narrative context of the meditation. This is indeed one of the main points of interest in the *Meditations*, for, as Mikhail Bakhtin says:

> Meanwhile, the true object of inquiry ought to be precisely the dynamics of these two factors, the speech being reported (the other person's speech) and the speech doing the reporting (the author's speech). After all, the two actually do exist, function, and take shape only in their interrelation, and not on their own, the one apart from the other. The reported speech and the reporting context are but terms of a dynamic interrelationship.[177]

As Bakhtin also points out, this interrelation is especially important because it reflects the society in which it functions. Hence, an analysis of the ways in which the *Meditations* apprehend the Bible will provide not only an understanding of the poetics and structure of the work itself, but also important insight into d'Aubigné's, and his fellow believers', religion in its private and devotional as well as public and political dimensions.

Bakhtin proposes two fundamental tendencies that govern the relationship between the narrative discourse and the reported discourse. The first he calls the "linear style," which deals with the Other's discourse ("le discours d'autrui") as a compact, impenetrable whole, establishing clear boundaries between it and the narrative discourse. For the opposite tendency, the "pictorial style," the frontiers between the two discourses are less rigid and the narrative context can infiltrate, to a more or less degree, the reported discourse. The linear style thus shows a dogmatic, clearly hierarchical conception of social interaction, whereas the pictorial style reflects a more individual-oriented, personal approach.[178] In analyzing the interrelation between the author–meditator's voice and that of God in the *Meditations*, one finds that it is not static throughout but contains elements that cover the spectrum between the

---

[176] This is not to deny the influence of what Bakhtin calls the *discours d'autrui* in the Bible; but the psalms do not contain the same type of meditation expressed in the prose psalm meditations.

[177] Bakhtin/Voloshinov, *Marxism*, p. 119.

[178] Bakhtin/Voloshinov, *Marxism*, pp. 120ff.

two styles proposed by Bakhtin. The three main modes governing the relationship between the two discourses in the *Meditations* are (1) a linear apprehension of the Bible as supreme authority; (2) an apprehension of Scripture that is both linear and pictorial, reflecting more personal interaction; and (3) a pictorial apprehension of the Bible in which the individual is clearly affirmed and even rivals in some senses the original authority of Scripture. These styles, which are manifested in the appropriation of the Bible in the realms of seeing and saying, overlap in the *Meditations*, manifesting a complex relationship between the author–meditator's voice and that of God.

The Linear Style

One of the major modes governing the relationship between d'Aubigné's own discourse and that of the Bible is the linear style. The most striking indicator of this type of relationship is seen even before one enters into the text of each meditation. d'Aubigné places the entire text of the psalm at the beginning of each meditation. The usual practice was to preface the meditation with the first few words of the Latin version of the psalm. Jean de La Ceppède is the only other author who places the text of the psalm before his own text, but with this notable difference: they are his paraphrase translations. d'Aubigné, on the other hand, reprints the psalms from the Geneva Bible of 1569, and this difference with La Ceppède is capital. Although the Protestant Church had no official single translation that held the same authority as the Vulgate in the Catholic Church, there were nonetheless some accepted translations largely used by the Protestant believers, among which was the Geneva Translation. Although prose paraphrases of the psalms similar to La Ceppède's were common among Protestants and in no way considered any less valid, d'Aubigné's use of the Geneva Bible denotes a connection with the official Church structure of Protestantism. It also underlines the "closeness" to the original text that was so important to d'Aubigné. By placing these psalms at the beginning of the *Meditations*, d'Aubigné visually establishes the primacy of the biblical text within the economy of the meditations.

The same type of relationship, in which the biblical text dominates by its mere textual presence, is also evident throughout the meditations themselves as a result of d'Aubigné's extensive use of italics. Not only does the text of the psalm appear at the beginning in italics, but also within the body of the meditation itself when it is quoted, so that one can see how the psalm is disseminated in the text. These quotations, either that of the psalm or of another biblical passage, vary in size. At times there is such an extensive quotation that it continues for almost a complete page, sometimes representing a passage even longer than the original psalm of the meditation. At other times, the author quotes just one or two verses together, and in still other passages he puts only certain words in italics. Furthermore, at several points in the *Meditations*, d'Aubigné complements the use of italics with marginal notes indicating the sources of the italicized text when it does not come from the psalm. Not only does this reinforce the fact that these elements have been incorporated from elsewhere, but it also refers the reader–meditator to this other discourse in a very direct manner, surrounding the text of the meditation with a "foisonnement" of other biblical texts that, by their sheer number and size, subsume the discourse of the meditation. It is as if d'Aubigné wants to make absolutely sure that it is clear that his text is a "secondary" text, insofar as it is based on another, previous word.

In addition to quoting the Bible extensively, d'Aubigné also speaks about the psalm and the Bible as a whole in the *Meditations*. It has already been shown how he establishes the superiority of the Bible in the preface, making it clear that there is no human discourse that can rival its authority. There is also specific mention of the Bible in the *Meditations*, as in the meditation on Psalm 16, where d'Aubigné says:

> Si cette puissance et bonté de Dieu conjointes à bien faire, à partager cet heritage, de la mention duquel les livres saints sont remplis, font choses miraculeuses. . . . (P. 563)

Elsewhere, he makes explicit reference to the psalms. For example, in the meditation on Psalm 16, he writes,

> Nous avons un familier exemple de cela au raisonnement de David avec son Dieu, qui argumente ainsi avec lui en plusieurs de ses Cantiques: *J'ai mis nom esperance en toi, garde moi donc, Seigneur*, ou bien: Je suis à toi, mets moi a sauveté. (P. 558)

As with the marginal references, these comments not only establish d'Aubigné's meditation as a commentary on the psalms, but once again refer the meditator back to the Book of Psalms and the Bible as the source from which the meditations flow. This is clearly seen at the beginning of the meditation on Psalm 16: "Mais sur tout le Pseaume XVI, s'attache à cette preuve dés le commencement jusques à la fin, amplifiant les graces vrayement gratuites . . ." (p. 558). This comment, which comes at the outset of the meditation on this psalm, sends the reader immediately back to the psalm and effaces the text of the author of the meditation behind an exegesis of the biblical text.[179]

---

[179] The whole paragraph in question is a sort of summary of the text that follows, and thus beginning with "Pseaume XVI" as the subject of "s'attache à cette preuve," the amplification of

Another means by which d'Aubigné establishes the priority of the biblical text is by speaking of its authors, which not only calls attention to the text he is dealing with, but also places the author of the meditation in a position of necessary inferiority to the original author. d'Aubigné often makes explicit mention of David, or "le Psalmiste," as he leads the reader in a reenunciation of his words. In the meditation on Psalm 16, he speaks of the "poëte sacré":

> sous cette houlette nous possedons la graisse et les plaisirs de la terre. . . . jusqu'aux parfums et delices specifiés par nostre poëte sacré, dans lesquels, comme il dit ailleurs, nous sommes rassasiés de moëlles et de friandises. (P. 562)[180]

The rather obvious allusions to Psalm 23 are completed by the reference to the poet, and the term "spécifiés" is like a footnote referring the reader to the psalms that can and must complete d'Aubigné's text. In other instances, the author uses the term "prophet," which underlines the divine inspiration of what is being quoted. At the end of the meditation on Psalm 84, for example, he writes, after a quotation, "Ce sont les termes du Prophete, et pour finir comme lui au Pseaume présent, Bref Dieu tresfort, heureux je croi/ L'homme qui s'appuye sur toi" (p. 570). Placing this at the very end of the meditation effectively silences the voice of the author and refers the reader to the book of psalms as the final word, providing a sort of "ouverture" that surpasses the meditation itself.[181]

At several points in the meditations, d'Aubigné's text magnifies specific words or phrases of the psalms. In the meditation on Psalm 84, d'Aubigné gives an extended commentary on the words "soleil" and "bouclier" from verse eleven and shows how they both represent different aspects of the way in which God deals with his children. In the meditation on Psalm 133, he makes a significant digression concerning one word:

> Ces benedictions se peuvent bien appliquer à plusieurs sortes de compagnies, mais plus particulièrement et veirtablement à l'Eglise, et aux familles de l'Eglise: car le Prophete en reserrant cette beatitude à

God's grace that comes is a natural result of the psalm itself and not really the work of the meditation author.

[180] d'Aubigné uses very similar imagery in the meditation on Psalm 84 when describing the difficulties of persecution: "Nous ramassons curieusement et à leche doigt les miettes du man celeste, que nous laissions pourrir sous les pieds, en l'extremité de nostre desolation. . . . En l'amertume de pareilles complaintes, nous cueillons des fleurs au Cantique du Prophete Royal que n'avions pas remarquees auparavant" (p. 510).

[181] A similar example is found in the meditation on Psalm 16, where a quote from Psalm 57 is followed by the phrase "Et ce qui s'ensuit" (p. 566), which again brings a whole other psalm into the text of the meditation, subordinating it to a fuller discourse.

Sion designee par LA, en frustre privativement Moab et Amalek, etc. (P. 505)

Interestingly enough, the adverb "LA" is not present in the translation of the psalm quoted at the beginning of this meditation (it is, however, in the Geneva translation, and as Henri Weber notes, "il s'agit probablement d'une coquille de l'edition").[182] d'Aubigné, nonetheless, places a great amount of importance on this one word, and his rendering of it in capital letters within the meditation amplifies the minute attention he pays to it. For him, every single word of Scripture plays an essential role in the transmission of the overall message of the Kingdom, and in this instance he sees the LA as a syntactical representation of the foundational doctrine of predestination.

The subordinate relationship of the meditation to God's discourse is also seen in another way, which d'Aubigné sums up thus: ". . . mais voici une autre procedure, qui est de l'escole de la Foi." Indeed, the notion of "school" is an extremely important one in the *Meditations*, for the meditator needs the instruction and guidance of God in order to say things correctly. This is seen in the vocabulary used to introduce many biblical citations: "nous apprenons à psalmodier à nostre Dieu (p. 565)," "Nous apprenons à prononcer avec le Prophete cette sentence . . ." (p. 561–62), "Puisque ta parole nous instruit" (p. 546), and "Il faut un grand soustien et secours de l'esprit de Dieu pour pouvoir dire de la pensée comme de la bouche . . ." (p. 523). In these instances the Word of God is that which comes in and aids the believer. The operative force behind this is God's grace:

> Aprés la grace de Dieu nous a donné l'asseurance, et nous a fait dire, *Nostre pere qui es és cieux*, aprés la seconde qui nous a fait suivre, *Ton nom soit sanctifié, ton regne advienne, et puis Ta volonté soit faite.* (P. 562)

God's grace thus empowers the meditator to pray that which he is simply incapable of praying by himself: total submission to God's will for the advancement of the Kingdom. In this way, the words that come out of the mouths of the believers are a sure sign of their election and the work of God in their lives:

> certes, il semble que les enfans de Dieu soyent lors trés mal partagés, et toutefois (qui est un mystere incomprehensible à l'homme animal) c'est là où nous disons: L'Eternel est la part de mon heritage et de mon breuvage; tu maintiens mon lot. (P. 562)

The work of the spirit of God in redeemed man—here opposed to the unredeemed, "l'homme animal"—produces speech that is a mystery to the world.

---

[182] Weber, notes on d'Aubigné's *Meditations*, p. 1256.

The enunciation of these words represents a work of God who in this manner speaks through his children.

In the examples seen up to this point, the reported speech of Scripture, in both its physical textual presence and the author's self-effacing submission to it, is clearly dominant. It is almost as if the author did not exist. He is, however, the one behind this arrangement that so highly exalts God's voice. His role in this process is not always tacit, and at many points in the text he makes his presence felt more. In this variant of the linear style, the author, while still holding himself in submission to the Word as the supreme authority, plays a more active role in the transmission of the message of the Word, acting in many ways as a preacher instructing the faithful. This is seen first of all in the preface. On the one hand, the author seems to focus mainly on his decision to publish the meditations and offer them to the public, and not really on his role as author. In this way his role is that of simply putting Scripture on display, so that Scripture itself will have the effect only it can achieve. On the other hand, the very title "l'Autheur au lecteur" points to the existence and role of the author of the meditations, and the first line of the preface makes it clear—"Plusieurs diverses occasions m'ont excité aux Meditations que ce livret vous presente . . ." (p. 493)—it is a question of *his* meditations. Thus, although he insists that the Bible is superior, that the Bible changes lives, and that the Bible allows communication and communion with God, he is nonetheless an active agent in this process: "j'ay estimé estre à propos de faire voir . . ." (p. 493), and "c'est assés que par cette Epistre je convie mon Lecteur à eslever ses pensées à Dieu . . ." (p. 494). The demonstration of the Bible's superiority and the opportunity to commune with God are thus in some way attributable to the author's efforts.

The exact nature of the author's role in this process is revealed in the *Occasions et Arguments* that precede the meditations, in which d'Aubigné explains why he wrote each text. For the most part he focuses on the psalm. The full title of the "occasion" always contains the psalm, so the first one, for example, reads: *Occasion et Argument de la meditation faicte sur le Pseaume CXXXIII*. In addition, in the majority of cases in the *Occasions*, d'Aubigné makes explicit mention of the biblical text. In the *Occasion* explaining the genesis of the meditation on Psalm 84, for instance, he says that the meditation is in response to the chagrin of a friend "ce Pseaume fut choisi pour consoler et conseiller ce Seigneur" (p. 508). Here, there is no mention of the meditation at all, only the voice of the psalm is important, and the author's only task was to choose the psalm. In the *Occasion* for Psalm 73, however, he writes: "nostre autheur fit present à ses amis de cette piece, qu'il estima propre à leur consolation" (p. 521). This time there is no mention of the psalm, and although it is implicitly present, the focus here is on the "piece" of the author, which he presents as a gift and considers consoling. The link between these two is explained in the *Occasion* for the meditation on Psalm 16, where, in response to the death of a friend "l'Autheur . . . ayant pris les fleurs du Pseaume 16 pour matiere de sa consolation, la mit depuis en ordre pour en faire present à ses amis" (p. 557). This statement makes it clear that the author's work does not involve any *inventio*, for the "matiere" comes only from the Bible. The author's skills do, on the other hand, come into play where the *dispositio* is concerned. His role is thus not to be ignored, but it is still totally subservient to the power of the divine Word.

The meditation on Psalm 73 contains a clear example of the relationship between the divine *inventio* and authorial *dispositio* in the realms of both seeing and saying. In the scene in question, the elect see a vision of a "fille" in front of the Sanctuary. The image of the Sanctuary here is representative of God's dwelling place, and so in coming to it, led by an Angel, the elect are seeking after God: "En ces saisons de desolation l'Ange consolateur meine les esleus frapper à la porte du Sanctuaire, à ce grand cabinet des secrets de l'Eternité" (p. 528). Their arrival is immediately contrasted with another image, that of the cherubim with the flaming sword forbidding Adam to reenter the Garden after he tried to make himself equal with God by eating of the fruit of the forbidden tree. Such pride and selfishness are not like the humility of the elect who are seeking "instruction ou consolation." They are described in terms of the humble ones who were interpellated by John the Baptist's message: "quand ils demandent les paroles de vie, et comme à Saint Jean, qui estoit l'Ange envoyé de Dieu: Maistre, que ferons-nous?" (p. 528). The identity of the elect is thus totally defined in terms of biblical personages.

Such is also true for the "femme," who appears twice in the episode. In the first part she looks worn and haggard and delivers a long complaint, fearing that she has been abandoned by God. Her first appearance is described in the following manner:

> Les enfans de Dieu, estans à l'huys du Sainct des Saincts, voyent arriver une femme, bien que claire, brune de son soleil qui la regarde de tous costés, d'une parfaite beauté, qui avoit ses vestements deschirés, ses cheveux brunis, couverts d'un sac et parfumés de cendre. . . . (P. 528)

The "femme" in question is obviously the one from the first half of verse one of Revelation chapter 12: "Un grand signe parut dans le ciel: une femme enveloppée du soleil. . . ." d'Aubigné has added several elements to this image to make it fit into his schema. The rest of this passage in Revelation goes on to speak of the woman being pregnant with a male child, and she is chased by a dragon wishing to devour the child. d'Aubigné does not mention that, but he does translate the atmosphere of the flight from the dragon in his description of the woman. He paints a picture of one in great distress, signified by the torn clothing; the sackcloth and ashes are an Old Testament sign of mourning. After voicing her complaints, the "fille" disappears behind a cloud of incense, and then reappears "avec un visage aussi gay que desolé auparavant, recouverte de vestemens neufs et candides, une couronne d'estoiles sur son chef, en sa main un livre scellé de plusieurs seaux . . ." (p. 530). Here d'Aubigné brings in the rest of verse one of Revelation 12: "Un grand signe parut dans le ciel: une femme enveloppée du soleil, la lune sous ses pieds, et une couronne de douze étoiles sur sa tête." These elements were obviously left out of the first description of the girl, because they give a sense of triumph that the author wanted to reserve for this section of the harangue. He intensifies this notion of triumph by making a curious addition to the image: the book with the seven seals. In the book of Revelation, only the Lamb who was slain (Christ) is found worthy of opening the book with the seven seals, because he "has overcome." d'Aubigné certainly does not equate the woman with Christ, but rather in this manner reinforces the triumphant message of the second part of the speech. In this it is evident that d'Aubigné's material comes from the Bible, but he exercises much liberty in dealing with this material.

In any case, the image of the woman seems to be of only preliminary importance as a preparation for what she will say after both of her appearances. Before her first speech, d'Aubigné writes "quelque desolee qu'elle fust, et tourmentee en son courage, elle n'avoit rien diminué de sa majestueuse gravité, le respect de laquelle empesche la troupe de passer le sueil; et elle seule l'ayant franchi prononça la harangue qui s'ensuit . . ." (p. 528). What follows this statement is of special importance concerning the harangue: "de laquelle elle fit les virgules de souspirs, et les points de sanglots redoublés" (p. 528). Such a description makes one think of this speech in terms of a text, which is exactly what it is, because, for the most part, it is a series of quotes, paraphrases, and references to various parts of Scripture. The first paragraph is composed of allusions to Psalm 45. The next is composed in three quarters of citations from various psalms, and then a section comparing the woman to Job—"Tu as desployé sur moi les flots de ta tempeste, et les mesmes rigueurs qui ont mis ton serviteur Job sur le penchant du desespoir" (p. 529)—which is followed by another paragraph continuing this reference to Job and adding a few more allusions to other biblical episodes. The next two paragraphs continue the lament with several direct references to biblical texts, and then finally the first part of the harangue ends with two paragraphs of quotes from the psalms, expressing the woman's dismay before the seeming abandonment of God.

The second section is a bit more didactic than the first part, for the woman is no longer speaking to God, but now to the elect. Although not with the same intensity as in the first part of the speech, she communicates her triumphant message with the help of some psalm quotations and references to biblical stories (such as the circumcision of Moses' son). She ends with a passage that, by referring to both Old and New Testament images, brings the past and the present together in an anxious expectation of the future:

> Quittez joyeux ce qui sent la bouë et la terre; quittez sans regarder à regret Sodome bruslante, car il vous faut aspirer, et bien tost parvenir à la couronne celeste qui fleurit à l'Eternité. (P. 532)

In the end, the seemingly audacious invention of this scene is based completely on biblical images, and it turns out to be a means of bringing in more biblical text in order to communicate the spiritual message more effectively.

The author's concluding remarks are helpful for understanding his conception of the relationship between the reporting context and the reported speech: "Voila les enseignements de la fille du Ciel, des oracles du sacré lieu, qu'il vaut mieux recevoir par les mains de l'Eglise que par les contes que nous faisons de nos doigts" (p. 532). The first line points to the narrative structure, the framework he, as author, has constructed for the scene. Even there, however, the focus is not totally on himself, for, as we have seen, this "fille" is not a purely fictional construct. In addition, the emphasis is on her *enseignement*, and not on the "fille" herself. Moreover, calling the teaching "des oracles du sacré lieu" equates them with the very words of God, which, as he explains, must come from the church, whom she obviously represents. Thus, in the final analysis, the "fille" disappears, and only the teaching remains. That is not at all to deny the efficacy of the narrative framework, but it is obvious, when one considers what follows it, that this elaborate dramatic image is a means of making the believer wake up to his or her wrong judgment and follow the example and instruction of the Church. The narrative framework is an artful work of *dispositio*, but it is still submissive to the efficacy of the divine *inventio*.

The meditation on Psalm 133 demonstrates another way in which the author makes his presence clearly felt while remaining submissive to God's voice. The *Occasion et argument* for the meditation says:

> depuis le Roy mesme ayant convié l'Autheur à monstrer qu'il deposait bien quelquefois l'humeur cynique, à faire quelque piece sur les douceurs de la paix, cette-ci fut choisie, où il y a des choses qui sentent la contrainte, et quelque difference en l'usage de la liberté. (P. 495)

The major concern here is not about the psalm but about d'Aubigné: the question is whether or not he can write something about peace, and the psalm has been chosen for a meditation to prove that he can do just that. Moreover, he makes it clear from the outset that his treatment of the psalm might be, or indeed is, different from what is expected, which again points to his role in the whole process. Although the psalm and its inherent qualities are not ignored, there is a decided emphasis on the "autheur" in this case.

However, once into the meditation itself, it becomes evident that although the authorial voice is strong, it still remains in submission to the Scriptures. Psalm 133 is about the sacralizing of the priest, and from this image d'Aubigné develops an allegorical representation of the body politic. First, he concentrates on the body of the priest and is able to develop a picture of society. Then, basing his interpretation on a passage from Deuteronomy that explains how the oil is to be mixed, d'Aubigné arrives at a recipe for the correct functioning of society.[183] He immediately follows this with the statement:

> mon lecteur prene en bonne part un partage que je fais ici sans authorité expresse de l'Escriture, pour en tirer quelque doctrine, et des consequences propres pour convier à leur devoir ceux que nous ne pouvons y contraindre. (P. 499)

Thus, after what is the most audacious of his dealings with this psalm in this meditation, d'Aubigné makes sure it is clear that it is he who is speaking on his own. He states his own goal and hopes it will accomplish his wishes, but he does not confuse it with the divine teaching of Scripture.

One finds, then, that the statements in the *Occasion et Argument* of Psalm 133 concerning the author were not so much meant to valorize his own inventions—although they are not ignored and are considered valid—but instead to make a clear demarcation, once again, between the reporting speech and the reporting context. In her book *Subverting the System: D'Aubigné and Calvinism*, Catherine Randall-Coats sees d'Aubigné's treatment of this subject matter as "a flagrant violation of Calvin's injunction against allegory."[184] However, given the care that d'Aubigné takes to point out what he is doing in order to guard the reader from falling into any possible misinterpretation that

---

[183] "Or est-il à considerer, qu'en la confection de cette liqueur celeste, le chef seul à qui il appartient d'offrir la Myrrhe, contribuë d'un tiers à sçavoir de cinq cens sicles, et emporte seul autant que l'Eglise et la Noblesse: au premier desquels nous approprions la cinnamome, et à l'autre le roseau aromatique, pour portion des peuples nous laisssons la Casia de mesme poids" (pp. 498–99).

[184] Catherine Randall-Coats, *Subverting the System: d'Aubigné and Calvinism*, vol. 16 (Kirksville, M.I.: Sixteenth Century Essays and Studies, 1990), p. 41.

the author's own poetic license might engender, it hardly seems to be a flagrant violation of anything, but instead a cautious advancement into possibly dangerous territory. Moreover, Randall-Coats seems to overlook an important part of the passage from the *Institution* that she quotes. Calvin says, "les allégories ne doivent estre receues sinon d'autant qu'elles sont fondées en l'Escriture. . . ."[185] There is no total injunction against allegory; only those that have no foundation in Scripture are forbidden. On this point d'Aubigné turns out to be more cautious than Calvin himself, for in his own commentary on this psalm, the Genevan pastor interprets the psalm as an allegory, and not as a "straightforward recounting of the historical sacralizing of the priest, Aaron," which Coats insists is all that is contained in the psalm. Furthermore, although the allegorical interpretations of Calvin and d'Aubigné are not identical, they are very similar on many points. Thus, Calvin himself felt that such an interpretation of this psalm was "fondée en l'Escriture." d'Aubigné's remarks thus make him seem all the more cautious; far from flaunting his authorial powers, he submits himself to the authority of Scripture once again by making sure that the reader is aware of any points where his own voice might be stronger than God's.[186]

This type of relationship with the biblical text is indicative of a deep reverence for the Word of God as supreme authority. Whether the narrator totally effaces himself or submits his artistic talents to the message of the Word, a definite hierarchical relationship is maintained, and the Bible remains superior as the "sceptre royal, par lequel il nous gouverne comme son peuple."[187] The *Meditations* are a concrete example of submission to God's majesty as it shines forth and exercises power through Scripture, and they show how the Huguenots totally defined themselves with respect to this higher authority. In addition, the *Meditations* also show, in the picture of society they paint, that, given the intimate links between the spiritual authority of God and the temporal authority of the king, this definition also applied to the Huguenots' relationship with the King of France. As d'Aubigné says in his *Debvoir mutuel des roy et des subjects*, the reign of God and that of the king are "deux choses tres unies," and this link is manifested in the description of the monarchy that d'Aubigné gives in the meditation on Psalm 133, which, as the first meditation

---

[185] Calvin, *L'Institution, Livre V,* p. 90.

[186] The subjects, verbs, and object pronouns that d'Aubigné uses are also indications that he is giving his own interpretation: "*Nous posons* que la tiare *soit* le type du Roi, et *laissons* encore pour lui les yeux et le front; le reste du visage, la barbe et le col *nous represente* l'Ecclesiastique; les bras et la ceinture . . . *seront* pour la Noblesse; les jambes et les pieds *nous signifient* le people . . ." [emphasis added] (p. 499).

[187] "Au Lecteur," *La Bible qui est toute la saincte escriture,* p. iir.

of the collection, underscores the importance of the political overtones of the work.[188] Through the images of the body of the High Priest and Mount Sinai, he presents the king as the head of society who is to be reverently obeyed as God's appointed leader. Significantly, d'Aubigné describes a good king in the following way:

> A ces restaurateurs appartient de dire avec David: *Quand j'aurai accepté l'assignation, je jugerai droitement. Le pays s'escoulait, et tous cex qui habitent en icelui: mais j'ai affermi ses piliers. . . .* (P. 500)

The king is thus defined in terms of his own conformity to Scripture, which is manifested in what he says; that is, in his own submission and speaking of the "langage de Canaan." In the *Debvoir*, d'Aubigné makes it clear that it is this conformity, manifested in his "foy et serment," that forms the basis for the people's trust in and obedience to him.[189] Hence the people's submission to God through his Word is not only reflected in their submission to the king and his word, but is actually realized in part through the latter. For this reason d'Aubigné finds "l'estat de la Royauté le plus honorable et excellent de tous."[190]

The Linear and Pictorial Style

In the society pictured in the meditation on Psalm 133, the appropriation of the king's discourse, and consequently of God's, is a very submissive appropriation, in that it is recognized that the king is the one closest to God and as such is the head from which all blessings are to be evenly distributed: "heureuse compagnie de ceux le Roy desquels a accez aux choses hautes pour les digerer et distribuer" (p. 502). Yet the emphasis of this description of the king's duties goes beyond the hierarchical structure of society also to imply a more active, personal participation on the part of the one appropriating the authoritative discourse. "Diriger" and "distribuer" involve all the aspects of the meditative process: a rumination on, and mastication of, the object of meditation in order to understand it in all its fullness, followed by an application of what is learned in the appropriate areas. In the meditation on Psalm 133, the king is responsible for "distribution" going from "à la Province, à la Ville, à la famille et en fin à la personne particuliere . . ." (p. 497). This

---

[188] d'Aubigné, *Du debvoir*, p. 484.

[189] Commenting on tyrants, d'Aubigné says: ". . . quel malheur c'est au Prince, quand aprés les premieres perfidies il ne peut plus appaiser par sa parole, et luy faut cercher autre monoye que la foy et le serment" (p. 480).

[190] d'Aubigné, *Du debvoir*, p. 473.

distribution, going from society as a whole to the individual, reflects the process of digestion that precedes it. In addition, the transition from one part of society to the next also underscores the fact that everyone has a role to play in this process, for in d'Aubigné's picture of the body politic, although the king is responsible for the original digestion of God's power and blessings that come through his Word, they can only pass from one level of society to the next if each sector does its part and passes it on.[191] The various groups in society as well as the individual must actively appropriate divine power and blessing as passed on by the king.

In the second half of the meditation on Psalm 133, d'Aubigné makes its clear that the representation of society he gives is a reflection of spiritual truths.

> Or, comme les benedictions spirituelles sont non seulement principales, mais celles qui meritent ce nom, toutes nos doctrines doivent tendre directement à ce qui est de la gloire de Dieu, nous tournerons toutes ces similitudes à leur vrai but, commençans par là, que l'origine des faveurs du Ciel qui descoulent sur nos testes agit premièrement en nos coeurs. (P. 503)

In this section of the meditation, he echoes the same notion of appropriation as in the first half, this time applying it to "dans les Royaumes et Provinces, ou dans les familles, soit en la conscience d'un chacun particulier" (p. 504). The "digestive, distributive" appropriation d'Aubigné speaks of, which still rests on the authority of the Bible but involves a more personal direct apprehension of it, constitutes the second major variant of the interrelation of the narrative and reported discourses in the *Meditations*.

This type of interrelation is manifested first in the way d'Aubigné assimilates the biblical text in his own prose. A verse from the psalm or from another part of the Bible is often introduced by the verb "dire" or a similar verb; or d'Aubigné often begins a paragraph with a quote of a verse, and then the rest of the paragraph is a development or amplification of that verse. Either way, the biblical text is clearly set off from the rest of the text. At many points, however, the demarcation is not as clear, and the biblical text and d'Aubigné's

---

[191] "C'est aprés aux Ecclesiastiques . . . à sacrifier prieres à Dieu, à conferer leurs remonstrances et exhortations aux Princes pour la paix publique, et par l'exemple de leur probité à ramener les parties esgarees à la recognoissance et observation de leur devoir.

Le Noble y contribuë son sang, et faut que l'amour de sa patrie lui face avaler doucement, que lui, qui sert au corps de bras, envoye toute la graisse au ventre, et mesme aux parties qui n'ont part à son honneur, n'ayant pour son partage que l'employ de sa vertu, l'exercise de leurs espees et de leurs lances. . . .

De muscles et de nerfs est estoffé le peuple bas. . . . Le peuple doit estre content de participer en son ordre à ces odeurs excellents; car bien qu'il porte tout, si est-il le dernier qui contribuë au soin du public, et la partie de dessous les pieds est la plus esloignee du peril" (p. 500).

own words are fused together. This happens in varying degrees throughout the *Meditations*, first depending on the punctuation used. In the meditation on Psalm 84, he writes:

> A ce labeur plein d'esperance, le Ciel, se rendant partisan de nos desseins, se liguera pour eux, les arrousera, les emplira de ses pluyes, faveurs et benedictions: *Et tout pour avoir dit à Dieu, Tu es ma retraite*. . . . (P. 514)

In this case the colon marks off in a very manifest fashion the biblical verse, but it is not preceded by an introduction of any sort, so it appears as a continuation or explanation of d'Aubigné's own words. In the meditation on Psalm 16, the author goes a step further when he writes:

> nous employons nos amitiés et affections, non pour assister aux pervers, *mais aux saints qui sont en la terre, et aux gens notables d'icelle, ausquels je prens tout mon plaisir.* (P. 560)

Here the comma is a matter of syntax and has nothing to do with the fact that the clauses come from different sources. This type of absorption of the biblical text is even more evident in the following passage from the meditation on Psalm 133:

> Cette annee qui est, en sa felicité sur toutes les parties et sur toutes choses tant generales que particulieres, tesmoignage le plus exquis des graces de Dieu, preuve que sa paix est faicte avec nous, qu'il a *lasché les prisonniers d'Israël*, et que nos pechez sont remis. . . . (P. 497)

Here, the biblical text is not set apart in any way, and the grafting of this text onto d'Aubigné's sentence reflects the appropriation that comes through it, for it is a textual expression of the Huguenots' identification with the Israelites.

Even when the text of the psalm is incorporated in such a manner in d'Aubigné's prose, the use of italics still makes it stand out. The presence of Scripture in the *Meditations* is not always marked by italics, however. Very often in the *Meditations* one finds a word for word rendition of a specific verse, although there is absolutely no indication that the prose is taken directly from the Bible. In the meditation on Psalm 84, for example, commenting on verse seven of the psalm, d'Aubigné writes:

> Ce sont les pas et les progrez de la foi, qui est l'eschele de Jacob, et laquelle ne confond point en la tribulation mesme, mais porte patience, la patience l'espreuve, et l'espreuve l'esperance. (P. 513)

This is more or less a word for word quote of Romans 5:3–4.[192] At other points, d'Aubigné rearranges various verses as he works them into his text. Such is the case for the description of idols given in the meditation on Psalm 16:

> Cette jalousie monstre ouvertement que l'indifference et la fade dou-ceur ne peuvent convenir à un enfant de Dieu, en ce qui transfere sa gloire aux choses muettes, sourdes, aveugles, manchottes, et qui sont oeuvres des mains de ceux qui les adorent. (P. 561)

This is a reworking of Psalm 115:4–8.[193] In addition, in yet other places, d'Aubigné takes only a small part of a verse and puts it in a new context. In the meditation on Psalm 84, combining Jesus' teaching on the Kingdom from Matthew 11:12 and the warning to the church in Laodicea from Revelation 3, he writes:

> ces seins qui ne sont saincts ni Temples, mais cloaques d'eaux puantes et de laschetez, ont changé les violences, par lesquelles leurs peres ont ravi le Royaume des Cieux, en tiedeurs que Dieu vomit de sa bouche. . . . (P. 511)[194]

---

[192] "Bien plus, nous nous glorifions même des afflictions, sachant que l'affliction produit la per-sévérance, la persévérance la victoire dans l'épreuve, et cette victoire l'espérance." A similar case is found in the meditation on Psalm 51, where, speaking of the power of God's hand, it is written,

> "C'est elle encore qui reconcilie toutes choses à soi, ayant fait la paix par le sang de la croix: et ceux qui estoyent estrangers de Christ et estoyent ses ennemis en leur entende-ment, prests à toute mauvaise oeuvre, ceux-là réconciliés au corps de sa chair ont esté rendu saincts, san tache, et irreprehensibles devant Dieu" (p. 542)

This is from Colossians 1:22:

> "Et vous, qui étiez autrefois étrangers et ennemis par vos pensées et par vos mauvauses oeuvres, il vous a maintenant réconciliés par sa mort dans le corps de sa chair, pour vous faire paraître devant lui saints, sans défaut et sans reproche. . . ."

[193] "Leurs faux dieux sont or et argent, ouvragge de mains d'hommes. Ils ont une bouche, et ne parlent point; ils ont des yeux et ne voyent point. Ils ont des oreilles et n'oyent point. . . ." A more striking example is from the meditation on Psalm 73, a passage that comes from the com-plaint of the "fille du Ciel":

> "Est-ce le doüaire d'un mariage si haut? Sont-ce les habits si richement brodés, desquels je devais estre si precieusement attournee? Où est cett' union prospere, pour laquelle je devoye laisser de si bon coeur pere et mere? Où est l'or d'Ophir, et les riches presens de Tyr? Où sont ces beaux et nobles enfans qui devoyent estre Rois triomphants sur la terre?" (p. 528)

This is all a reworking of several verses of Psalm 45 (cf. Weber, notes on d'Aubigné's *Medita-tions*, p. 1263): v. 10: "Filles de roi sont entre tes dames d'honneur: ta femme est à droite, parée de l'or d'Ophir;" v. 13-15: "Et la fille de Tyr, et les plus riches des peuples te supplieront avec des présents. La fille du roy est toute pleine de gloire: son vestement est semé d'enchasseures d'or. Elle sera présentée au roy en vestments de broderie . . ."; and v. 17: "Tes enfants seront au lieu de tes peres: tu les establiras pour princes par toute la terre."

[194] Matthew 11:12: "Depuis le temps de Jean-Baptiste jusqu'à présent, le royaume des Cieux est forcé, et ce sont les violents qui s'en emparent." Rev. 3:15–16: "Je connais tes oeuvres. Je sais que tu n'es ni froid ni bouillant. Puisses-tu être froid ou brouillant! Ainsi, parce que tu es tiède, et que tu n'es ni froid ni bouillant, je te vomirai de ma bouche."

The following reference to Matthew 4:4 in the meditation on Psalm 16 embodies both the mechanics and the function of this type of assimilation:

> Certes lors nous nous moquons des moqueurs, et mesprisons les mesprisans, qui ne sçauroyent comprendre comment l'homme ne vit point de pain seulement, mais de toute parole procedante de la bouche de Dieu. (P. 562)[195]

d'Aubigné's rendition of this verse in itself constitutes the "moquerie" he speaks of, for the way he incorporates this verse, and many others, into his own prose shows the extent of his understanding that his spiritual life depends totally on God's word. Unbelievers are not even able to grasp the message he is conveying because they cannot recognize the "langage de Canaan" of the author's discourse.

This applies to an even greater degree on yet another level. Although the references to the Bible in the *Meditations* that are not pointed out by d'Aubigné are still obvious to those very familiar with the Bible, there are, in many other instances, only faint echoes of various verses. In the meditation on Psalm 84, for example, the phrase "Ce sont beautez qui ne fleurissent point pour estre fenees et flestries sur le soir," is reminiscent of Psalm 90:5–6,[196] and in his description of his sin, "Je n'apporterois que pechez sur pechez, car les meilleures actions de l'homme sont ordes et puantes comme le flux de la femme," d'Aubigné recalls words of the prophet Isaiah.[197] Likewise, d'Aubigné's request for forgiveness in the meditation on Psalm 51,

> . . . et à la fin efface de tes tablettes mon procez pour retourner à ton oeuvre encommencee, assavoir la perfection de mon salut: puis que ce que tu as une fois commencé et advancé tu ne le delaisses point. (P. 540)

This is reminiscent of Colossians 2:14 and Philippians 1:6.[198]

In addition to such cases, the meditations are full of biblical language and expressions. God is called the "Pere de lumière," "Soleil de Justice," "O Tout Puissant," "Tout Puissant créateur de l'univers," and "le Dieu des armées." Christ is referred to as the "Fils de ta dilection," and the "bien aimé Fils."

---

[195] "L'homme ne vivra pas de pain seulement, mais de toute parole qui sort de la bouche de Dieu."

[196] Cf. Weber, notes on d'Aubigné's *Meditations*, p. 1257: " . . . au matin c'est comme une herbe qui se change. Laquelle fleurit au matin et reverdit; le soir on la coupe et elle se fane."

[197] Isaiah 64:6: "Nous sommes tous comme des impurs, et toute notre justice est comme un vétement souillé."

[198] Colossians 2:14: "Il a effacé l'acte dont les ordonnances nous condamnaient et qui subsistaient contre nous . . . ;" Philippians 1:6: "Je suis persuadé que celui qui a commencé en vous cette bonne oeuvre la rendra parfaite pour le jour de Jésus-Christ."

Satan is the "ennemi de nostre salut." God's children have been "racheté par la mort du Fils," and "sanctifié par le sang du Sauveur." The end of times is referred to as "la grande journée du Seigneur," and the descriptions of heaven are replete with cherubims and seraphims, and the elect will receive a "couronne de gloire." In this manner, the apprehension of Scripture in the *Meditations* is a complete one, beginning with the biblical text as a whole, seen in the placement of the psalms at the head of the meditations, and then proceeding to deal with it in smaller and smaller units, going from verse to phrase to specific words. In the end, the text of the Bible has been thoroughly incorporated on every level in the narrator's discourse, ranging from quotation of long passages to faint echoes of various terms or images. Through this saturation of biblical passages, themes, images, and vocabulary, the *Meditations* bring alive the whole universe of the Bible as it applies to the meditator.

Bringing it alive for the meditator in this way implies, as in d'Aubigné's conception of society in the meditation on Psalm 133, an active participation of those receiving it. This is also seen in the *Meditations*, as summarized in the following passage from the meditation on Psalm 16:

> Où sont les enfans du siecle qui osent dire en le croyant, que les Anges ayent un camp planté alentour d'eux . . .? Prendront-ils pour eux ces propos excellents? (P. 565)

It is an apprehension based on an identity—seen in the contrast with the "enfans du siecle"—and on faith, for the teachings of the Bible must be approached with confidence that they are true, and in this way they can be personally appropriated. This is reflected first of all in some uses of the "saying" vocabulary. As seen above, the meditator is led into a reenunciation of the "langage de Canaan" by the grace of God and the ministry of the Holy Spirit. In other places, however, the meditator takes a more active role in the reenunciation. For example, in the meditation on Psalm 84, he writes, "Il faut dire de toutes nos affections, si nous voulons que ce soit avec efficace" (p. 513). In this case it is the meditator who must muster up all of his affections and faith in order to make his reenunciation an efficacious performance. d'Aubigné continues:

> Pour reprendre ce bon vouloir, nous ne saurions si tost dire, *Il faut confesser à Dieu nostre mesfait*, qu'aussitost l'Eternel n'ait osté la peine de nos pechez: et voilà le desespoir changé en esperance, l'ignorance en doctrine, et l'inconstance en fermeté. . . . (P. 513)

The meditator sees the need to restore his will, and so rushes to the Word, and the result is immediate—his will is restored and he is reconciled with God.

Furthermore, the meditator, fully aware of his sinfulness but at the same time of his privileged position before God, often introduces his words with the verb "oser." For example:

> ils n'oseroyent dire à Dieu en foi comme nous,
> > Veuille sous l'ombre de ton aile
> > Me garder bien seuremnet. . . . (P. 565)

Also:

> Là parmi nos imperfections et foiblesses nous osons dire:
> > Quelques assuts qu'aye senti
> > J'ai toujours tenu ton parti. (P. 561)

In these instances the meditator asks for God's protection and then makes a declaration of being on God's side in spite of his infirmities, which would seem to disqualify him. Through this "daring" he brings the truth of the Word into his life, receives God's protection, and becomes a true partisan of God's cause.

The active participation of the meditator in the "langage de Canaan" is also seen by the inclusion of the meditator in the story of the psalm. This is already a part of the definition of the meditation genre, which is based on paraphrase and application; but d'Aubigné's texts make this highly evident. The first paragraph of the meditation on Psalm 133, and thus the first paragraph of the whole collection, sets the tone: "Voici le souverain bien . . . mais le *voici* (qui est à dire) present de lieu . . . nous contente et dit *Voici*" (p. 496). Here, the author makes it clear that the truth of the psalm is seen in the present; it is not simply an anterior word, but one that is immediately applicable. A similar instance of this is found in the meditation on Psalm 88, in which it is written: "Eternel, Dieu de ma delivrance, ou mieux, de mes delivrance, qui m'as tant de fois tiré du bas tombeau de la mort . . ." (p. 548). The first line is a direct quotation of the first line of the psalm. The addition "ou mieux . . ." is not in any way meant to be an improvement on the words of the psalm, but rather is a statement of the continual reapplication of it. The truth of God's deliverance is multiple—"tant de fois"—and always present.

The applicability of the Scriptures to the present is greatly facilitated by the use of the biblical "je" and "nous." Fragonard, in her *Pensée religieuse*, takes opposition to Michel Jeanneret's point of view, by claiming that the references to the present in the *Meditations* are only actualized by translating the allegories present in the text.[199] In some cases she is correct, as in the following example:

---

[199] Fragonard, *La Pensée religieuse*, vol. 1, p. 75.

Voila un autre vestement, et une autre liqueur que celle d'Aaron, pour les ennemis de paix. Tous les autres foudrayantes menaces sont de par Dieu le salaire des oeuvres de *nos* adversiares qui *ont persecuté*. . . . (P. 504)

Here the "nos" is an appropriation, but it is sufficiently generic so that it does not necessarily apply directly to the Huguenots without, as Fragonard says, an interpretation and translation of the situation into the present. There are, however, many points in the text where the appropriation to the present is clear and there is really no need for a translation. In the meditation on Psalm 133, for example, near the end of the comparison of mounts Zion and Hermon with the state, d'Aubigné writes:

Nous avons veu la pratique de telles choses en ce Royaume affligé . . . C'est de là que nous avons veu les palais changé en masures, les galeries de Fontainebleau en estables, les jardins en pasturages, les fontaines en soüil de porceaux et la Sale du Louvre en gibets. (P. 502)

With the mention of Fontainebleau and the Louvre, the author brings the eternal truths of the examples of the Bible alive in the present. What is happening in France is because of its participation in the eternal verities contained in the Bible: "c'est de là." The lives of sixteenth-century men thus fit into the spiritual history of humanity as recounted in Scripture. This is even more evident in a passage from the meditation on Psalm 51:

C'est cette main qui fait tant de merveilles sans peine, qui abbat du throsne les orgueilleux et tire de la boüe le pauvre gisans sur terre, pour le colloquer aux honneurs du peuple de Dieu, et de mesme tire un Joseph de la prison pour lui donner en main les resnes d'un Royaume, les libertez de ceux qui le tenoyent captif, et la vie qui disposoyent de la sienne. A quoi nous attacherons les examples de Henri quatriesme en France, et en Angleterre d'Elizabeth. (P. 542)

The same hand that was active in the life of Joseph is the one that has protected Henri's and Elizabeth's; their lives join in the succession of all of those whom God has brought to power in order to further the purposes of his Kingdom on earth. With the "a quoi nous attacherons . . ." the author brings together the past and the present as equal instances of the working out of God's power and the establishment of the Kingdom.

The assimilation of the biblical text to the present is also apparent in the way d'Aubigné emphasizes the spiritual interpretation of different passages. Take, for example, his treatment of the image of the temple in Psalm 84. The psalm begins "Eternel des armees, combien sont aimables tes tabernacles!" A description follows of the psalmist's thirst for the tabernacle of God and the blessings of those who reside in it. In his commentary on this psalm, Calvin begins with a discussion of the historical circumstances surrounding it, and then later arrives at the following conclusion: "The end he had in view in desiring so earnestly to enjoy free access to the sanctuary was, that he might there worship God with sincerity of heart, and in a spiritual manner."[200] d'Aubigné's treatment of the image is completely in accordance with Calvin's interpretation:

> Voila la cause violente de l'amour sans mesure que nous portons à tes parvis, o Dieu, et nos ames pantelantes les vont cerchant, comme la biche des eaux: elles defaillent en cette recerche, et se pasment en leurs desirs enflammez, lors mesmement que les mechants qui n'ont point d'yeux pour le Temple spirituel, demandent: où est la demeure de nostre Dieu? (P. 510)

However, d'Aubigné begins his meditation with this interpretation, without considering the immediate circumstances of the original composition of the psalm. Calvin laments those who "would understand by the tabernacles of God, the kingdom of heaven as is David mournes over his continuance in this state of earthly pilgrimage . . .,"[201] and d'Aubigné's spiritual interpretation comes close to such an understanding. However, d'Aubigné's meditation does not concentrate on the Kingdom of God to the exclusion of its connections with and manifestations in this life. Rather, as clearly seen in the *Occasion et Argument*, he simply anchors the spiritual significance of the psalm to another specific historical situation.[202]

In the meditation itself, d'Aubigné applies the image of the temple to contemporary circumstances by comparing his fellow believers with those of the first years of the Reformation:

> Ces seins qui estoyent sanctuaires, ces coeurs tables de la Loi, et sur lesquels elle estoit escrite du doigt de Dieu, ces estomacs, cabinets des thresors de constance, ont fait ouyr mesme dans les feux les magnifiques paroles du Dieu vivant. Ces premiers Temples ont esté abbatus par la mort, et en leur honteuse posterité nous ne voyons que masure, retraites de serpents et de lutins, de vices et d'infections. (P. 511)

Referring to the tablets of stone on which God inscribed the ten commandments on Mount Zion, d'Aubigné bases his contrast on the notion of fullness

---

[200] John Calvin, *Commentary on the Book of Psalms*, trans. Rev. James A. Anderson, vol. 2 (Grand Rapids: Baker Book House, 1984), p. 354.

[201] Ibid., p. 352.

[202] In response to the complaints of a friend, "ce Pseaume fut choisi pour consoler et conseiller ce Seigneur, et ceux que pareille amertume de coeur afflige journellement" (p. 508).

and emptiness. Former believers had remained faithful and obedient to the commandments of God and thus in their devotion to him. In their distress, what came out of their mouths was a reflection of the fullness of their heart. d'Aubigné's contemporaries, however, had empty hearts—"Ces coeurs affadis que Dieu a laissé fondre en les abandonnant, pource qu'il en estoit abandonné" (p. 511)—and thus they were full of nothing but ruin. The equation of individual hearts with the image of the Temple is especially significant in that it shows the degree to which d'Aubigné has appropriated the psalm for sixteenth-century readers, for it is based on a New Testament idea. d'Aubigné has obviously taken Paul's teaching on the individual believer as the temple of God, and woven it into the image from the psalm.[203]

The rest of the meditation involves a restoration of the Temple on every level. First, the believer must ask God to work in his heart and "refais en des Temples, remets y ton Arche, l'Urim et Thumim, et tire encore dehors des nephtars et purifications" (p. 512). d'Aubigné here applies Old Testament symbols to the New Testament conception of the individual temple. The request is for God's presence, symbolized by the Ark of the covenant, and for God's guidance and wisdom, symbolized by the Urim and Thummim.[204] After this textual restoration of the individual spiritual temples, the author returns to the image of the Temple as the presence and dwelling place of God. He says: "et au lieu que nos iniquitez et infidelitez nous avoyent fait perdre de veuë le pinacle du Temple sacré, nous aurons le feu pour guide en nostre nuict . . ." (p. 513). The emptiness of heart is equated with distance from the outer temple, and the restoration of the inner one thus brings a rapprochement to the outer one. As the meditation continues, the believer moves closer and closer to the dwelling place of God. After seeing the Temple again on the horizon, "Ton esprit nous apprene d'estimer plus les cachettes seures de ton Temple qu'estre haut montez és tabernacles d'iniquités" (p. 515). Finally, near the end of the meditation, he says "nous avons trouvé à quoi attacher nos desirs: c'est au pavois de l'Eternel, où nous trouvons la cachette sans honte et l'eslevation sans peril" (p. 520). Thus, from sight, to estimation, to a deep longing, the meditation uses the image of the temple to bring the believer closer and closer to God. Most importantly, this has been done not on a purely abstract spiritual level, but, by applying the framework of the psalm to

---

[203] I Corithians 6:19: "Ne savez-vous pas que votre corps est le temple du Saint-Esprit qui est en vous, que vous avez reçu de Dieu, et que vous ne vous appartenez point à vous-mêmes?" and I Peter 2:5: "et vous-mêmes, comme des pierres vivantes, édifiez-vous pour former une maison spirituelle, un saint sacerdoce. . . ."

[204] Urim and Thummim were the precious stones that the high priests used in order to discern the will of God for the nation of Israel.

the current situation of the Religious Wars and by clearly relating the teaching of the psalm to Christianity through the introduction of the New Testament variant of the Temple image, d'Aubigné has brought the psalm "up to date" for his fellow believers. The closeness with God that results from the meditation is something that the meditator can experience "journellement"—as indicated in the *Occasion et Argument*—that is, in his particular daily circumstances.

The way in which d'Aubigné's meditation fosters intimacy with God through a present-day application of the teachings of the psalms manifests a personal approach to Scripture, one that recognizes and respects its authority, not in any way intimidated by it but appropriating it personally. The author–meditator of the *Meditations* does just that. For him the story told in the psalms is clearly his own and that of his contemporaries. This is seen in the "mirroring" vocabulary that d'Aubigné uses in his text. The individual mirrors God's grace as described in Scripture. When speaking of repentance in the meditation on Psalm 51, d'Aubigné writes:

> Restitue en moi la vie et la joie; refai moi tel que tu prenes plaisir à me regarder; et lors, moi miserable . . . et de voix et de coeur deviendrai un docteur de repentance, un miroir de ta grace, un eschantillon de ton pouvoir. (P. 541)

The effect of repentance and God's work in the life of the believer makes him a mirror of God's grace. This is made more explicit in another passage: "Sois mon Soleil, et moi ta Lune" (p. 516). Here, the believer is a source of light, but not of life; he is totally dependent on God's existence to give any meaning or definition to his own.

Although in some instances the believer reflects God's glory and majesty as revealed in Scripture, in others, Scripture is presented as a reflection of the Christian. Such is the case in the meditation on Psalm 84, when, after discussing a passage concerning the temple, d'Aubigné says: "Est-ce point un miroir de nostre condition aux persecutions dernieres . . ." (p. 512). This is also the case with the vocabulary of "portraits" and "pictures" throughout the text. In the same meditation the author writes: "O vous personnes particulieres . . . voicy le portraict de vos peines et de vos succez . . ." (p. 514), and in Psalm 73, after quoting a verse from the Psalm: "Voila un beau portraict de ce que nous voyons tous les jours . . ." (p. 524). In all these cases, the original is no longer the image from the Bible, but the lives of the believers. A portrait is that which is copied from the original, and so according to the logic of Psalm 51, the lives of the meditators should be the "portraict" of the stories of the Bible as they reflect the truth of Scripture as its verities are worked out again and again in their lives. In d'Aubigné's case, however, there appears to be a switch between the archetype and the type. Instead of the lives of the believers being types of the archetypal eternal truth laid out in the Bible, they are promoted to archetype, and the stories of the Bible to types of their truth.

"La suite des propos de ton Prophete ne sont-ils pas la description de mon estre, et la leçon de mes funestes propos?" This statement in the meditation on Psalm 88 embodies the reciprocal nature of the notion of reflection that is operative in the *Meditations*. On the one hand, the emphasis is on the meditator whose life is of primary significance, because the importance of Scripture comes from its ability to describe the individual's situation. At the same time, the Prophet's "propos" are held up as an example of universal significance. They contain the truth of the narrator's life, but they also reflect the truth of every person's life. Each one can come to the Bible and find himself pictured in it. The "propos" of the Prophet equal those of the meditator, the former serving as the "leçon" for the latter. There is full reciprocity between the believer and Scripture. The reverence due Scripture as God's authoritative Word does not exclude a very personal appropriation of this Word, and in this manner the importance of the individual as a child of God and the importance of Scripture are equally affirmed.

The Pictorial Style

The "digestion" of the Bible and the mirroring vocabulary in the *Meditations* are indicative of the infiltration of the reported discourse— Scripture—by the narrative discourse. When the author breaks down the biblical text and inserts himself and his fellow believers in it, Scripture is no longer an impenetrable, compact whole. The boundaries have weakened, and although the Bible remains God's authoritative Word, it is treated in a very familiar manner by the author–meditator. In the third variant of the interrelation between the two discourses in the *Meditations*, this familiar approach that valorizes the individual is sometimes taken a step further. The voice of the author–meditator becomes much stronger, sometimes even to the point of rivaling the authority of Scripture. This is seen first in instances in which d'Aubigné goes beyond the work of *dispositio* and enters into the realm of *inventio*. The picture he paints of the devil in the meditation on Psalm 51 is a good example of this (cf. p. 5). The image of Satan as a painter gives an accurate account of biblical teaching concerning his activities, but it is nonetheless d'Aubigné's invention. Another example of this is found in the meditation on Psalm 16, in which d'Aubigné contrasts Christians with nonbelievers.

Telles differences paroissent entre les bestes ravissantes qui vivent de proye et de sang, et les douces et innocentes, desquelles la vie n'esteint point d'autre vie, et les boyaux n'avallent point les entrailles d'aucun gibier. Les premiers animaux devorent vilainement, jettans les yeux à gauche et à droite au soupçon des tripailles, menacent et grondent pour estre effroyable, tout en peur, tout en fureur; et mesmes les loups mordent l'eau au lieu de l'avaller doucement: d'autre costé les petits poulets, les colombes et autres oyselets, ayans saucé le bec en l'eau, levent la teste et les yeux en haut; et regardez leurs paupieres, elles font contenance d'action de graces vers le ciel. (P. 556)

These images are certainly in no way heretical; they serve as a metaphor for the truth that d'Aubigné is trying to express. They come, nonetheless, not from Scripture but from d'Aubigné's own poetic arsenal, and thus they point to his own creative activity.[205]

d'Aubigné also strengthens the weight of his own discourse by bringing in examples from sources usually considered incompatible with Scripture. He himself condemns the "fables" of men in the meditation on Psalm 133,[206] and yet in the meditation on Psalm 88 he uses such a "fable" to make a point:

Les Anciens ont inventé que leurs Erynnes, ou Furies estoyent filles du Soleil et de la Nuict: voulant à leur mode figurer, que les affaires pesantes de la journee tormentoyent les affligés dans le nid des pensees, et au loisir de la nuict. C'est sous elle que la memoire me gehenne, ma couverture est de plomb et mon chevet d'espines. . . . (P. 549)[207]

---

[205] It must be noted that although there are numerous instances of this in the *Meditations*, they are a small minority in comparison with the hundreds of images d'Aubigné takes from the Bible.

[206] "Il n'est point ici question de feindre un amour fabuleux, ni une vaine Deité conciliatrice des accords discordans. Vous ne verrez point ici le fils de Pore et de Penie employé à rejoindre l'Androgene separee par le couteau de l'Absence, en portant à l'une et l'autre nature la reunion qui mit le Ciel en jalousie. Arriere les fables de nostre verité . . ." (p. 496).

[207] Although the inclusion of this example in the *Meditations* does point to the author inasmuch as it comes from a source outside the Bible, it is not that surprising of a phenomenon, according to Marie-Madeleine Fragonard, who says (concerning the *Tragiques*, but her point also applies to the *Meditations*): "si les textes profanes y figurent, ce sera en tant qu'ils peuvent constituer une representation du sacré, même si là n'est pas forcément leur intention première," and "il ne nous semble pas qu'un esprit du XVIe siècle doive y voir d'incompatabilité" (*Essai sur l'univers religieux d'Agrippa d'Aubigné* [Mont-de-Marsan: Editions InterUniversitaires, 1991] pp. 47, 63). In the meditation on Psalm 16, d'Aubigné attributes some truth to philosophers: "Les philosophess Ethniques ont bien sçeu dire, que la derniere mutation ne nous change qu'en nous mesmes . . ." (568), but their knowledge only applies to earthly truths: "si cela par la cognoissance des Payens s'est peu dire de tous corps humains . . ." (p. 568), and not at all to spiritual truths: "Si, di-je, on a jugé la duree de l'homme sur ces marques, que peut-on dire du chrestien, duquel l'eritage est surceleste?" (p. 568).

The verb "inventer" shows that he believes their explanation to be false, but he treats it nonetheless as a poetic expression of truth, "à leur mode." Moreover, he also treats his own production as a poetic expression of truth, for at several point in the *Meditations*, he quotes *Les Tragiques*.[208] When speaking of the conscience in the meditation on Psalm 88, for instance, he cites a passage from *Feux*:

> Le meschant une fois arresté en cet estroit chachot, encor qu'il eust à son commandement la compaigne, porte la geole avec soi, et les ceps de sa coulpable pensee galopent avec lui.
> Cette prison le suit, quoiqu'il coure à la chasse,
> Quoi que mille pays comme un Caïn il trace,
> Qu'il fende au gré du vent les fleuves et les mers,
> Sa conscience n'est sans cordes et sans fers. (P. 551)

This passage itself contains a direct reference to the Bible, but it is d'Aubigné's own invention. By incorporating it into the *Meditation*, d'Aubigné gives it a status similar to that of the biblical passages he quotes.

A second, more intimate way in which the author–meditator's voice comes to rival that of God is by questioning God's authority. This questioning can be directly related to the political circumstances of the Religious Wars. It must be remembered that d'Aubigné's meditation on Psalm 133, which contains the portrait of a peaceful, well-administrated society, was written after the Wars, in 1607. Fragonard insists that, even then, the image of the body politic in that meditation is "fondé sur l'éloge des Idées plus que sur les faits, semble un refuge contre la réalité et contre l'Histoire."[209] For the most part, and especially during the earlier years of the period covered by the *Meditations*, the Huguenots believed that they had more than sufficient reason to question the way the King was fulfilling his role. Their questioning was practically manifested in the vast production of literature addressing the issue of sovereignty—where it comes from and whether it has any restraints. In principle, the King's shortcoming were seen as his own failure to keep the covenant he made with God, a failure that did not in any way affect the believers' covenant with God. However, in examining the relationship between the narrative discourse and that of the Bible in the *Meditations*, it appears that

---

[208] The *Tragiques* are quoted nine times in the *Meditations*. Four times there is no introduction, but in the other cases the quotation is introduced in a way similar to the Bible quotations: ". . . ausquels on dit . . ." (p. 506), ". . . de laquelle on a escrit . . ." (p. 517), ". . . de laquelle il est dit . . ." (p. 525), "auquel est apporté cette comparaison en ces termes . . ." (p. 534), and ". . . dont nous lisons en quelque lieu . . ." (p. 571).

[209] Fragonard, *La Pensée religieuse*, vol. 1, p. 311.

the type of "mise en question" of the earthly king actually at times spilled over into the Huguenots' relationship with the heavenly King. In several instances, the voice of the meditator is no longer only in submission to God's discourse but instead enters into a dialogue with it, apparently on equal footing. In some instances the voice of the meditator seems to question divine authority in order, as d'Aubigné himself puts it, "entrer en conte avec Dieu."

This is seen, for example, in the meditation of Psalm 73. There the author follows the general contours of the psalm while amplifying the complaint element of the text in a way that gives a strong voice to the anguish and confusion of the meditator. The psalm itself recounts the amazement of the believer when he sees that the wicked continually prosper while he continually suffers, and it makes him question his commitment to God. Why try to live righteously when all it brings is persecution? Are not the wicked to be envied? However, when he enters the sanctuary of God, the psalmist understands that his afflictions are only temporary, while those of the wicked will one day be eternal. He therefore repents of his shortsightedness and continues to trust in God in spite of the way things appear. The voice of God totally triumphs over that of man in the end. This is also what happens in the meditation, but in a way that gives full vent to the voice of anguish and complaint that is in the psalm. At first it appears that d'Aubigné is almost ashamed of the complaining in the psalm, and he feels the need to explain it:

> Mais Dieu aura pitié des affligés pour son Nom, il excusera chacun fidele disant avec angoisse, Voila, ceux ci sont meschans, à leur aise en ce monde, ils acquirent de plus en plus de richesses. . . . (P. 526)

The address here seems to be triple: he is speaking to God, to himself, and to the reader. The quotation from the psalm, audacious because it questions the goodness and authority of God, is excusable in the meditation, because it is said out of anguish, which keeps the believer from thinking correctly. Moreover, this anguish is the result of the believer's faithfulness to God, for it is in his name that the trouble is being experienced, and therefore God will, and indeed must, excuse it.

At the same time, d'Aubigné's development of this verse serves to downplay the audacity of this way of addressing God, while also allowing him and the reader to voice their own confusion and complaint in a way that does not involve blasphemy. This becomes even clearer in the next paragraph of this meditation, which continues the believer's complaint. Again, the author excuses the words of the anguished believer in the way he presents his words, something that is of course not done in the psalm itself. He begins "Ils passent outre s'escrians, Quoi que ce soit, c'est en vain que j'ai nettoyé mon

Coeur . . ." (p. 526). They are thus beside themselves, and in a certain sense they themselves are not speaking. He then continues, "et aprés plusieurs sortes de telles protestations, avec une punition juste qui est demeuree attache, l'affligé ose dire: A la mienne volonté que j'eusse qui m'ouyst . . ." (p. 526). Here again he seems upset by the audacity of these words and so he adds "une punition juste"—which is totally undefined, but nonetheless magnifies the complaint—introducing this audacity with the verb "oser." The quotation that follows is the high point of Job's contest with God, when, after remaining faithfully silent for so long, he decides that he is justified and that God is wrong in his dealings with him, so he demands an audience with God. The use of this verse here is thus highly significant, for it is not a question of dealing with one of the verses of the psalm itself—one that possibly has to be explained away—but rather is one that has been purposefully chosen to give full vent to the inner turmoil of the meditator. The text chosen reveals the depth of the strife and confusion that exists.

This confusion is also seen in the narrator's attitude toward God and Satan. When describing the wicked, the psalm says:

> Pour cette cause, orgeuil les environne comme un carquan, et accostrement de violence les couvre. Les yeux leur sortent dehors de force de graisse: ils surpassent les desseins de leur coeur.

d'Aubigné says:

> Mais encor n'et-il point estrange que Dieu supporte la prosperité des ennemis, comme l'orgeuil qui vient de prosperité, et les blasphèmes qui viennent de l'orgeuil: car il les environne d'un carquand, et accoustrement de violence les couvre. Vous diriez que par cet accoustrement l'Esprit de Dieu veut designer les carquans que plusieurs ont obtenus à la persecution de l'Eglise, la plus part sans merites militaires, mais les ayant receus pour couronnes de leur graisse et de leur orgeuil. . . . (P. 524)

d'Aubigné's text is somewhat more vehement toward God than the actual text of the psalm, which in no place actually comes out and speaks of God as in any way responsible for the prosperity of the wicked. The meditation author, on the other hand, calls this "estrange," and, moreover, reconstructs the text of the psalm in a way that makes God the subject of the verb "environne," making it look as if God himself were actively supporting the wicked in the sense of giving them support. As for Satan, the author says: "Enfin il a falu esclatter plus avant: car Satan, qui ne perd aucune occasion de nuire, nous dicte de plus furieuses leçons, et apprend ces textes à l'affligé: "Perisse le jour auquel je naquis . . ." (p. 526). Once again he quotes Job in his anguish, and this time it is an extremely long passage. It seems almost paradoxical that Satan, the conquered one, should be allowed so much space. Hence, once again, there is an ambiguity in the meditations. The author is dealing with the voice of the complaint that is present in the psalm, but he has an almost confused reaction to it. He believes it to be sinful, and he thus attributes it to Satan. At the same time, however, he expands upon it. The resonance of the complaint has resonated deeply within the author, and he thus deals with the reported speech in a way that allows him to express fully this deeply felt reality.

In the end, the voice of God triumphs over that of man: "A tels exces de douleur, il est bien besoin que l'esprit conservateur s'oppose en destruisant, et dicte aux esleus nouvelles pensees, et un chant de repentance . . ." (p. 527). The meditator repents of his murmuring and complaints and once again totally submits himself to God. However, even in the vocabulary of this last statement, one perceives an openness to the murmuring voice of the meditator. The phrase "A tels exces de douleur . . .," presents the meditator's complaints as the result of outside circumstances; the believer is led to question God, almost legitimately, because of what he is experiencing. Thus, although the voice of God must come in and destroy and bring repentance, there is nonetheless a remarkable leniency toward this sin, which would seem to border on embracing it as acceptable. No virulent condemnation, no chastisement. Also, when one considers the fact that the scene of the "fille du ciel" comes after this episode, the permissibility that is attached to this type of complaint is reinforced, because in her speech she does exactly the same thing, and there is absolutely no attempt made to soften the voice of her complaining. It is loudly heard, and although at the end the meditator is led to repentance once again, he has been allowed to fully express himself, with the guarantee of having done it through biblical texts. At the end of the meditation, the meditator has indeed been brought to the same point of repentance and acceptance as that of the original psalmist, but not without having had the opportunity to express the innermost turmoil of his soul in a way that is not really present in the original text. Borrowing extensively from elsewhere in the Bible, the author permits the expression of self in a safe way.

The meditation on Psalm 73 thus gives significant weight to the narrator's voice. It does in the end submit to God's discourse, but not without making itself heard—more than once. The meditation on Psalm 88, written as an expression of d'Aubigné's grief and anguish upon his wife's death, goes a step further, and in this text the narrator's voice is given freer reign. Once again, the author follows the contours of the psalm itself, and the choice of the psalm is in itself highly significant, for, as opposed to Psalm 73, which ends in a sort of renewal that brings the psalmist back to God, Psalm 88 is one of total complaint, in that it does not contain any such "return" to God's vision of things. Thus, d'Aubigné's willingness to include such a psalm in his collection is already a statement in itself. It is not surprising that the meditation gives free reign to the author's distress, because that is what is contained in the psalm. This meditation is characterized, more so than the others, however, by paragraphs that begin with an italic quotation of one of the verses of the psalm, followed by a development/paraphrase/amplification of the verse that allows the author–meditator to restate it in his own terms. The author finds no need to soften or excuse the statements of the original psalm, but rather freely develops them.

Indeed, instead of thinking of his words as blasphemous in any way, in this meditation the words of complaint seem to be totally acceptable. d'Aubigné expresses this by a comparison between the meditator and Christ:

> Pardonne, Seigneur, puis que la mesme cholere attribuee et deployee sur l'agneau sans peché, quelque pur, juste et puissant qu'il fust, lui a fait dire: Mon Dieu, Mon Dieu, pourquoi m'as-tu abandonné, t'esloignant de ma delivrance et des paroles de mon gemissement? Mon Dieu, je crie de jour et de nuict, et n'ai point de cesse. Si le Fils de ta dilection, inseparable de sa divinité, a tremblé et jetté grumeaux de sang; si le Prince de vie a veu avec effroi le visage ridé de la mort, à quel poinct pourra demeurer le courage et l'esperance d'un miserable pescheur comme je suis, qui a de quoi s'escrier:
>   Mes jours passent comme un'ombre
>   Qui s'en va obscur et sombre. (P. 554)

Although he begins with "pardonne" and calls himself a "pescheur," these terms seem to be totally subsumed by the comparison with Christ. If the God-man, who never sinned—"inseparable de sa divinité"—voiced a complaint, what can be expected from mere man?

This license is in some way justified by the psalm itself, but d'Aubigné goes a step further. The comparison with Christ is just that, a comparison, and the meditator's life is definitely contained within the example of Christ's earthly life. However, at another point the author comes to contrast himself with David:

> David se plaignoit d'estre hors de la souvenance de ses amis, d'estre mis en oubli du coeur des hommes comme un mort, d'estre estimé autant qu'un vaisseau de nul usage: mais c'est bien pis d'estre comme mis en oubli de son Dieu, et retranché d'entre les vaisseaux à honneur, pour estre jetté hors le camp. . . . (P. 550)

Here, the words of the psalm are considered insufficient to express the meditator's experience. David's complaint is real, but the reality of the meditator's life is "bien pis." This is reinforced at the end of the meditation, where one reads: "je n'ay plus de paroles puissantes, ni assez violentes à l'expression de mes miseres" (p. 536). This comes after several quotations of various biblical passages, so it appears that the "langage de Canaan" has been exhausted: it is not even capable of expressing the depth of his misery. His own discourse—the pain he feels—has thus taken over; its strength is its expression.

In conclusion, from the inclusion of the psalm at the beginning of each meditation to the complaining voice of the meditation on Psalm 88, the *Meditations* display a wide range of interaction between the author–meditator and God. None of the variants, or the "styles" of interaction, can be limited to any particular text, although each one comes to the forefront at particular moments. It is true that the first and second variants presented above are more frequent than the third, but consequently the third variant stands out all the more when it does appear. The coexistence of these three styles reflects the complex nature of Huguenot faith and its literary expression. This complexity is perhaps best explained by considering the three variants of the interrelation between the narrative and reported discourses as a mixture of what Michel Jeanneret calls the two "styles religieux" of d'Aubigné: the "style a-littéraire" and the "style littéraire."[210] The "a-literary" style focuses solely on the biblical text and seeks to strengthen the reader's devotional life. The *Meditations* are clearly centered on the Bible, with the goal of bringing the meditator into closer communion with God. The literary style, on the other hand, allows for more personal artistic expression, giving the individual a greater value. This is also seen in the *Meditations*, for the work of the author is often highly evident, sometimes even to the point of eclipsing the biblical text. The author of the *Meditations* does not only write, however; he also meditates, and thus the focus on the individual in this text is also on the meditator, who accepts the Word of God as his or her own story and appropriates it in a very personal manner. Based on the identity "un enfant du Royaume," the individual carries on an intimate conversation with God, freely expressing all fears and pain. Much of this pain is due to the political turmoil of the Religious Wars, so the political implications of the "langage de Canaan" are not ignored—as seen in the meditation on Psalm 133. The interaction between the author–meditator and God often reflects interaction between the king and his subjects. For d'Aubigné, however, all things earthly pale in comparison with spiritual realities, and, in the end, the main focus of the *Meditations* is the individual believer's relationship with God, a relationship that will be sealed in the eternal Kingdom.

[210] Michel Jeanneret, "Les Styles d'Agrippa d'Aubigné," *Studi Francesi* 32 (1967): 246–57. Jeanneret speaks specifically of d'Aubigné's psalm paraphrases in this article.

IV

Conclusion

A PROTESTANT GENRE

d'Aubigné's *Meditations sur les Pseaumes* hold an important place in the literature of the late sixteenth century, for, as an expression of the faith of the Huguenots, they demonstrate the relationship between a specific set of Reformation beliefs and practices and a specific form of literature that embodies these beliefs and practices. This form of literature constitutes a locus for working out, in both its private and devotional as well as public and political dimensions, the faith of which it is an expression. The affinities between the salient characteristics of the prose psalm meditations and Protestant Bible reading practices are notable: the prose psalm meditations were much more of a natural outgrowth and expression of Protestant than of Catholic spirituality. The fact that a couple of Catholic authors also wrote prose psalm meditations precludes one from saying that this type of writing was uniquely the affair of Protestants. In general, the Protestant authors felt more "at home" in these meditations; their works are more elaborate, demonstrating an intimate interaction with the biblical text—as so clearly illustrated by d'Aubigné's *Meditations*—and the Protestant desire and capacity to delve into each psalm, to amplify and actualize its teaching, and to develop fully all the virtual meanings and applications of the passages.

The close relationship between Protestant beliefs and practices and this type of devotional writing leads to the following question: can one speak of a Protestant genre where these meditations are concerned? The answer is yes, if one adopts the Jaussian notion of genre as a group or family that is defined historically as the horizon of expectations, for the genre is continually being

113

founded and altered.[211] Within this framework one can say that during a particular period, these texts constituted and defined a specific genre, that of
prose psalm meditation. When the Protestant authors published these meditations, they adopted and revitalized an age-old genre; but, because they
linked this genre to Protestant spirituality, their works were new for their
times. When one examines the written meditations that immediately preceded the prose psalm meditations, which were manifestations of Catholic
spirituality, it is clear that the texts at hand were, for the most part, radically
different from what was expected in a written meditation at that time. Thus,
whereas prose psalm meditations did not present a great disparity with the
horizon of expectations in the sense that they only presented what the Protestants had been prepared for by their church and family life, as literary devotional texts—as opposed to the doctrinal expositions and the sermons that
prepared the audience for them—the texts went against expectations. They
resulted in a change of horizons by negating the type of meditative experience
fostered by the dominant Catholic meditations in order to give a literary
manifestation to Protestant spirituality.

This change of horizons had a definite function in Protestant devotional
life. The prose psalm meditations were written during the Reformation and
the early years following it, when Protestantism was still being established
and defined, and they played an important role in that process. These meditations did not simply restate the lived experiences of Protestant believers;
rather, while building on a certain knowledge of and familiarity with the
psalms, they served to increase this knowledge and familiarity, and especially
to encourage the application of the truths and teachings of the psalms. One of
the best examples of how these texts occasioned a change of horizons, which
involved both an aesthetic and a social function, is the notion of penitence in
Protestant spirituality. Rejecting the Catholic sacrament of penitence and
concentrating instead on the individual's private reconciliation with God, the
Protestant meditations' authors presented not merely mirrors of what was already happening in all Protestants' lives, but rather examples to be followed.
In this and other ways, the meditations fostered the private and personal
interaction with Scripture that the Reformers encouraged.

Dealing with these spiritual and devotional issues in the written meditations (in contrast to sermons, catechisms, and confessions of faith) naturally
posed the question of the relationship between faith and art. In the way they

---

[211] Hans Robert Jauss, *Toward an Aesthetic of Reception*, trans. Timothy Bahti (Minneapolis:
University of Minnesota Press, 1982). See esp. Chapter 3, "Theory of Genres and Medieval Literature" (pp. 76–109).

incorporate the biblical text, these works form a locus for attempting to answer the question of how spiritual truths may be expressed in literature. As d'Aubigné's *Meditations* clearly show, the answer is a difficult one, for there is a tension between a strict, very conservative adherence to the biblical text, on the one hand, and more relaxed poetics allowing human invention, on the other. More than purely a question of poetics, however, this tension is indicative of a larger issue. Mario Richter speaks of the intersection of a strict Christian view of art and the "irrésistible séduction exercée par la très riche imagination ronsardienne" in these texts, a "seduction" that was thus one of the times.[212] In other words, these texts demonstrate the struggle resulting from the desire to maintain a pure preaching of the Word and at the same time communicate its message in a way that placed it in the sixteenth-century context, which meant not jettisoning in toto the reigning poetics in the name of doctrinal purity. Hence, this tension and struggle are simply a part of the *Meditations'* attempt to bring alive the story of the psalms for the readers. In their confrontation and working out of these issues, the *Meditations* manifest a desire and endeavor to communicate and live out one's faith with doctrinal and devotional purity in a way that clearly relates it to the surrounding world.

In sum, the prose psalm meditations represented for these authors the means for expressing their faith, for it gave a literary manifestation to the already familiar form of their devotion. This literary form in turn gave voice to aspects of their spirituality—particularly how their faith was related to the context in which they were living it out—with which they had to wrestle. Prose psalm meditations certainly did not originate with these authors, but the examples they were building on, mainly from the Patristic age, were appropriated and developed by them in such a way that linked them intimately with Protestant devotion. These texts took on a very specific content, form, and style, as they existed alongside a more contemplative Catholic form of meditation, from which they were clearly distinguishable. Unwilling—and indeed unable—to adopt the dominant Catholic structure of meditation, Protestant authors turned to the form of prose Psalm meditations in an attempt to adequately articulate their faith in all of its ramifications, and in so doing constituted what can be called a Protestant genre.

A PROTESTANT CONSCIENCE

As an embodiment of the "langage de Canaan," the language of the Kingdom, the *Meditations* also embody the Huguenot identity so intimately

[212] Richter, "Apropos des 'Chrestiennes Méditations,'" p. 75.

intertwined with this language. Throughout the meditations the meditator is designated as the "enfan du Royaume," in opposition to "ceux du siècle." The distinguishing mark of this identity is the more direct, more immediate relationship with God that the "langage de Canaan" brings about. The "langage de Canaan" is thus the language of the individual conscience. For this reason, the "langage de Canaan" had vast implications, for it touched the very heart of the conflicts of the Religious Wars. It addressed the issue of the final authority with respect to which the individual should be defined. Placing the believer firmly within the Kingdom of God of course in no way negated his or her allegiance to the earthly king—in this case that of France—as the meditation on Psalm 133 so clearly shows. The basic foundation of that meditation, however, is that the earthly kingdom should be administered according to the spiritual precepts of the Kingdom of God, with the king himself "speaking" the "langage de Canaan." The other meditations however, in addressing the horrors and abuses of the king, claim that this was simply not the case. In response to this clear conflict of authority, in the *Meditations* the believer's only recourse is to appeal directly to God in the "langage de Canaan" with the hope of restoring religious and political purity in the earthly kingdom and with the assurance that even if the king's abuses do continue in this world, ultimate justice will triumph in the consummation of the Kingdom, hastened by the very act of speaking the "langage de Canaan." This recourse clearly establishes the supremacy of the individual conscience as a subject of God's Kingdom over that of a subject of any earthly authority.

Speaking the "langage de Canaan" thus established a clear hierarchy of allegiance by allowing direct appeal—"en simplicité"—to the ultimate seat of authority: God himself. The type of relationship with God made possible by the "langage de Canaan" also brought with it questions concerning the exact nature of the relationship between the believer and this final authority. The *Meditations*, in their first person appropriation of the biblical text, deal directly with these questions, which necessarily arose in the context of a religion that emphasized both the individual, with freedom of conscience, and the sovereignty of God. The *Meditations* embody this double emphasis and the resultant tension. This is seen first in the different stances the author takes vis-à-vis the psalm, ranging from a complete self-effacement to a manifest display of authorial invention. It is also evident in the meditator's expression of her or his emotions and struggles, which ranges from a complete acceptance to a dramatic questioning of God's sovereignty and care as expressed in Scripture. In the end, there is no neat resolution of this tension, for these tendencies coexist throughout the work, and the *Meditations* are thus the place where this struggle, inscribed in the very nature of a faith that concentrates both on the individual and God, is played out.

Although the meditations are a place of tension, they are, most of all, a place of confidence and assurance. In fact, the tension spoken of above is in many ways an outgrowth of this confidence and assurance that the meditator has concerning his relationship with God, which is manifested in statements such as "Dieu . . . prend plaisir que nous traittions avec lui comme de nostre droit" (p. 558). The "droit" in question is obviously that of the "children of the Kingdom" to which the "nous" refers, and this "treatment" is realized through the "langage de Canaan." Their ability to speak this language is first that which assures them that they are indeed subjects of the Kingdom— God's children—for the "enfans du siècle" are not even capable of recognizing it. Furthermore, the "langage de Canaan" assures direct contact with God, an assurance that undergirds the appropriation of Scripture in the realms of seeing and saying throughout the *Meditations*. The various ways in which the text of the Bible is incorporated in the narrative context of the meditations are thus textual expressions of this confidence founded on the identity of belonging to God and having him as Father. This is most poignantly manifested in the expression of the meditator's anguish and distress associated with the Religious Wars. In these instances the "language de Canaan" allows a safe, free-reined expression of the turmoil of the meditator's soul—like the many times Job is quoted along with the psalmist—and at the same time the "langage de Canaan" also assures the meditator of God's care and sovereignty in all of these circumstances. In this manner, the "langage de Canaan" provides total self-expression and also gives the confidence that this expression is permitted and heeded within the context of the Kingdom. Written in the language of the Kingdom, the *Meditations* thus firmly place the reader–meditator within the trajectory of the establishment of the Kingdom and constitute a locus for the manifestation and realization of the privileged relationship with God that the "enfans du Royaume" have.

The realization of this relationship in the *Meditations* comes through a double movement that, on the one hand, introduces the reality of the Kingdom in this world and, on the other hand, brings the meditator closer and closer to the fullness of the final stage of the Kingdom. In the meditation on Psalm 51, d'Aubigné makes the following request: "Et comme les pensees que tu me donnes sont arres et avant-coureurs d'un plus grand ottroi, meine mon esprit où ma foi et mes regards sont desjà volés, asçavoir au sein de ta grâce et au giron de tes douceurs" (p. 543). The term "pensees" harkens back to the preface, where d'Aubigné invited the reader to "eslever ses pensees à Dieu (en simplicité du langage de Canaan)" (p. 494). The two different sources of the "pensees" reflect the nature of the "langage de Canaan" in the meditations, for it is both God's "pensees," that is, his Word as contained in Scripture, and the meditator's "pensees," that is, Scripture appropriated by the believer to express himself through it. The communion with God that comes through the conjunction of these two forms an earnest of the future power and blessings of the Kingdom, allowing the believer to experience them in his present circumstances. As a result, the meditator finds himself between two worlds. This is poignantly expressed at the end of the meditation on Psalm 88: "je demeure extatique en mes angoisses, les genoux à terre, mes souspirs en l'air, mes yeux au Ciel, mon coeur à toi . . ." (p. 556). The dichotomy is clearly manifested here. The meditator is firmly entrenched in the difficulties of this world, the burden of which has driven him to his knees. That position, however, is also one of prayer and meditation, which lift him up to another world. This final phrase summarizes the very act of meditation of which it is a part, for in the meditation on Psalm 88, as in all the others of the collection, through the personal reenunciation of Scripture, the meditator gives free expression to himself in a way that brings him ever closer to the Kingdom.

The power of the language of this expression—the "langage de Canaan"—is such that it both prepares for and brings about the transformation that the believer will undergo in the consummation of the Kingdom—what d'Aubigné call the "heureuse mutation." The meditation on Psalm 16 says:

> Ainsi du contentement du coeur, et des exultations de la langue, la masse présente du corps apprends a s'asseurer: cette chair mesme qui trembloit de la mort en mesprise les menaces . . . et puis elle fait son esperance de ces désirs. (P. 567)

Through that which is spoken—the "exultations de la langue"—one's condition is changed from a state of fear into one of hope based on the desire of what is coming, and in this way the desire helps to bring about its own realization. Moreover, the "exultation de la langue" is also a part of the transformation, for as the meditator moves closer and closer to the fullness of the Kingdom in the *Meditations*, there is a transformation in his or her speech. As the meditator moves from the expression of pain to the expression of confidence in God, he or she goes from crying and saying to laughing and singing. The laughter is mainly about the judgment that will come against God's enemies, because the coming of the Kingdom will bring about ultimate justice. The singing comes from the joy of being accepted in God's family:

> Ce qui nous ravit en exultation vers le Seigneur, quand si mal partagés au monde, nous le sommes heureusement au Ciel, et chantons avec le

prophète, Que de bonté souveraine/Sa main droite est toue plaine. (P. 563)

Eventually, when the judgment and joy are both complete in the final phase of the Kingdom, the laughing and singing themselves give way to another way of enunciating the "langage de Canaan," one yet unknown, as seen in the final passage of the *Meditations*:

C'est là que nous parviendrons à ce que l'homme n'a peu supporter, à la lumiere inaccessible qui esblouyt les Cherubins de ses rayons, de laquelle la contemplation a donné le nom aux Seraphins: c'est cette splendeur insupportable que Moyse ne peut endurer, ni voir Dieu que par les parties de derriere, qui sont les effets de ses merveilles passees; et pour finir, c'est là où nous attend cette beatitude, qui n'a peu estre depeinte dignement, ni par la Majesté de Sina, ni par le splendide palais qu'Ezechiel nous a representé, ni par le glorieux estat de la Transfiguration, non plus par le portraict de celui qui parut à Sainct Jean entre les chandeliers, ni par l'estat excellent de la triomphante Jerusalem: c'est ce que nul oeil n'a peu voir, nulle oreille n'a peu ouyr, nul esprit n'a peu comprendre, et que nul coeur n'a peu desirer dignement. (P. 572)

In the end, thus, the dual nature of the "langage de Canaan" as manifested in the *Meditations*—that is, God's eternal Word expressed in the human language of Scripture and appropriated by the believers—will be simplified. In the Kingdom, there will be no dichotomy between present and future, material and spiritual, and there will therefore be a total correspondence between the signifiers and the signifieds of the "langage de Canaan." The mode of enunciation of the "langage de Canaan" in its pure form is thus foreshadowed, prepared, and ushered in by the various ways it is spoken in *Les Meditations sur les Pseaumes*.

Select Bibliography

Aubigné, Agrippa de. *Les Aventures du Baron de Faeneste*, in *Oeuvres*, edited by Henri Weber. Paris: Gallimard, 1969, pp. 669–830.

———. *La Confession catholique du sieur de Sancy*, in *Oeuvres*, edited by Henri Weber. Paris: Gallimard, 1969, pp. 573–666.

———. *Du debvoir mutuel des roys et des subjects*, in *Oeuvres*, edited by Henri Weber. Paris: Gallimard, 1969, pp. 467–89.

———. *Histoire Universelle*. 10 vols. Edited by Alphonse de Ruble. Paris: Librairie Renouard, 1886–1909.

———. *Les Meditations sur les Pseaumes*, in *Oeuvres*, edited by Henri Weber. Paris: Gallimard, 1969, pp. 493–572.

———. *Petites oeuvres meslees*. Geneva: P. Aubert, 1630.

———. *Poésies religieuses*, in *Oeuvres*, edited by Henri Weber. Paris: Gallimard, 1969, pp. 319–46.

———. *Sa vie à ses enfants*. Edited by Gilbert Schrenck. Société des Textes Français Modernes. Paris: Nizet, 1986.

———. *Les Tragiques*, in *Oeuvres*, edited by Henri Weber. Paris: Gallimard, 1969, pp. 1–243.

———. *Traité sur les guerres civiles*, in *Oeuvres Complètes*. 6 vols. Edited by E. Reaume and F. de Caussade. Paris: Alphonse Lemmerre, 1873–1892, Vol. 2.

"Au Lecteur," *La Bible qui est toute la saincte escriture, contenant le vieil testament, le nouveau testament; ou, la vieille & nouvelle alliance*. Geneva: François Iaquy, 1562.

"A Tous Vrais Amateurs de la Parole de Dieu, grace & paix par nostre Seigneur Jesus Christ," *La Bible qui est toute la saincte escriture, contenant le vieil testament, le nouveau testament; ou, la vieille & nouvelle alliance*. Geneva: François Iaquy, 1562.

Bakhtine, Mikhaïl. *Le Marxisme et la philosophie du langage*. Translated by Maria Yaguello. Paris: Editions de Minuit, 1977.

Bèze, Théodore de. *Chrestiennes Méditations*. Edited by Mario Richter, Collection Textes Littéraires Français. Geneva: Droz, 1964.

———. "La Confession de foi du chrétien." Edited by Michel Réveillaud. *La Revue Réformée. Soli Deo Gloria* 6 (1955).

———. *Du droit des magistrats sur leurs subjets*. Edited by Robert Kingdon. Geneva: Droz, 1970.

Bordier, Henri-Léonard. *Le Chansonnier Huguenot du XVIe siècle*. Geneva: Slatkine Reprints, 1969.

Bourdieu, Pierre. *Ce que parler veut dire*. Paris: Fayard, 1982.

Bovet, Félix. *Histoire du Psautier des Eglises Réformées*. Neuchâtel: Librairie Générale de J. Sandoz, 1872.

Brutus, Estiene Iunius [Philippe Duplessis Mornay]. *Vindiciae contra tyrannos* (1581). Edited by Henri Weber. Geneva: Droz, 1979.

Calvin, Jean. *Calvin's New Testament Commentaries*. Vol. 9, *The First Epistle of Paul to the Corinthians*. Translated by J. W. Fraser. Grand Rapids: Eerdmans, 1960.

———. *Commentaires sur l'Ancien Testament. Tome Premier: Le Livre de la Genèse*. Geneva: Labor et Fides, 1961, p. 58.

———. *L'Institution chrétienne*. 3 vols. Paris: Editions Farel, 1978.

Calvin, John. *Commentary on the Book of Psalms*. Vol. 2. Translated by Rev. James A. Anderson. Grand Rapids: Baker Book House, 1984.

Canons and Decrees of the Council of Trent. St. Louis: B. Herder Book Company, 1941.

Cave, Terence. *Devotional Poetry in France, 1570–1613*. Cambridge: Cambridge University Press, 1969.

Cayré, Fulbert. *La Méditation selon l'esprit de Saint Augustin*. Paris: Desclée de Brouwer, 1935.

Certeau, Michel de. *La Fable Mystique*. Paris: Gallimard, 1982.

Chaix, Henri. *Le Psautier Huguenot. Sa Formation et son histoire dans l'Eglise Réformée*. Geneva: Imprimerie Romet, 1907.

Chambers, Bettye Thomas. *Bibliography of French Bibles. Fifteenth- and Sixteenth-Century French Language Editions of the Scriptures*. Geneva: Droz, 1983.

Chartier, Roger. "Du Livre au lire," in *Pratiques de la lecture*, sous la direction de Roger Chartier. Marseilles: Rivages, 1985.

Compagnon, Antoine. *La Seconde Main, ou le travail de la citation*. Paris: Seuils, 1979.

Crouzet, Denis. *Les Guerriers de Dieu*. 2 vols. Paris: Champ Vallon, 1990.

Delumeau, Jean. *Naissance et affirmation de la Réforme*. Paris: Presses Universitaires de France, 1969.

Diefendorf, Barbara B. "The Huguenot Psalter and the Faith of French Protestants," in *Culture and Identity in Early Modern Europe (1500–1800). Essays in Honor of Natalie Zemon Davis*, edited by Barbara B. Diefendorf and Carla Hesse. Ann Arbor: The University of Michigan Press, 1993, pp. 41–63.

Dubois, Claude-Gilbert. *Mythe et langage au XVIe siècle*. Paris: Ducros, 1970.

Du Plessis-Mornay, Philippe. *Meditations chrestiennes sur quatre Pseaumes du prophete David*. Jacques Chouet, 1591.

Du Vair, Guillaume. *Meditations sur les Psaumes*, in *Les Oeuvres du Sieur du Vair*. Paris: Guillaume Loyson, 1618.

Estienne, Henri. *Discours merveilleux de la Vie, Actions & Deportemens de la royne Catherine de Medicis. Mère de François II, Charles IX, Henry III, Rois de France*. Paris: 1663 [1574].

Farel, Guillaume. *Le Pater Noster et le Credo en françoys*. Edited by Francis Higman. Geneva: Droz, 1982.

Fatio, Olivier, ed. *Confessions et catéchismes de la foi réformée*. Geneva: Labor et Fides, 1986.

Foucault, Michel. *Les Mots et les choses*. Paris: Gallimard, 1966.

Fragonard, Marie Madeleine. *Essai sur l'univers religieux d'Agrippa d'Aubigné*. Mont-de-Marsan: Editions InterUniversitaires, 1991.

——. "La Méditation sur les Psaumes: Monologue ou dialogue," in *La Méditation en prose à la Renaissance*. Paris: Presses de l'Ecole Normale Supérieure, 1990, pp. 89–104.

——. *La Pensée religieuse d'Agrippa d'Aubigné et son expression*. 2 vols. Lille: Atelier National de Reproduction des Thèses, 1986.

Frye, Northrop. *The Great Code. The Bible and Literature*. San Diego: Harcourt Brace Jovanovich, 1982.

Garrison, Janine. *Les Protestants au XVIe siècle*. Paris: Fayard, 1988.

Genette, Gérard. *Seuils*. Paris: Editions du Seuil, 1987.

Greenslade, S. L., ed. *The Cambridge History of the Bible*. Vol. 2, *The West from the Reformation to the Present Day*. Cambridge: Cambridge University Press, 1963.

Holt, Mack P. *The French Wars of Religion, 1562–1629*. Cambridge: Cambridge University Press, 1995.

Jauss, Hans Robert. *Toward an Aesthetic of Reception*. Translated by Timothy Bahti. Minneapolis: University of Minnesota Press, 1982.

Jeanneret, Michel. *Poésie et tradition biblique au XVIe siècle*. Paris: José Corti, 1969.

——. "Les Styles d'Agrippa d'Aubigné. " *Studi Francesi* 32 (1967): 246–57.

Kelley, Donald R. *The Beginning of Ideology. Consciousness and Society in the French Reformation*. Cambridge: Cambridge University Press, 1981.

La Ceppède, Jean de. *Meditations sur les Psaumes*, in *Les Theorèmes, suivis de Imitation des Psaumes de la penitence*. Toulouse: Colmiez, 1612.

Lazard, Madeleine. *Agrippa d'Aubigné*. Paris: Fayard, 1998.

Léonard, Emile G. *Histoire générale du protestantisme*. 3 vols. Paris: Quadrige/Presses Universitaires de France, 1961.

Les Meditations du zélateur de piété, recueillies des anciens peres. Paris, 1571.

Lestringant, Frank. *Agrippa d'Aubigné. Les Tragiques*. Paris: PUF, 1986.

Lewalski, Barbara. *Protestant Poetics and the Seventeenth-Century Religious Lyric*. Princeton: Princeton University Press, 1979.

Loyola, Saint Ignace de. *Exercices Spirituels*. Translated by Jean-Claude Guy. Paris: Editions du Seuil, 1982.

Marot, Clément. *Aulcuns pseaumes et cantiques mys en chant*. Strasbourg, 1539.

Mathieu-Castellani, Gisèle. *Agrippa d'Aubigné: Le Corps de Jézabel*. Paris: Presses Universitaires de France, 1991.

Mesnard, Jean. "Introduction," in *La Méditation en prose à la Renaissance*, Cahiers V. L. Saulnier, no. 7. Paris: Presses de l'Ecole Normale Supérieure, 1990, pp. 7–16.

Mesnard, Pierre. *L'Essor de la philosophie politique au XVIe siècle*. Paris: J. Vrin, 1952.

Montaigne, Michel de. *Essais*. Edited by Pierre Villey. 2 vols. Paris: Presses Universitaires de France, 1978.

Old Testament. London: Christopher Bakar, 1576.

Pallier, Denis. "Les réponses catholiques," in *Histoire de l'édition française. Tome I: Le Livre conquérant*. Paris: Promodis, 1982.

Pasquier, Estienne. *Choix de Lettres sur la Littérature, la Langue et la Traduction*. Edited by Thickett. Geneva: Droz, 1956.

——. *Recherches de la France*, in *Oeuvres choisies*. Geneva: Slatkine Reprints, 1968.

Pidoux, Pierre. *Le Psautier Huguenot du XVIe siècle. Mélodies et documents. Deuxième volume: Documents et bibliographie*. Bâle: Edition Baerenreiter, 1962.

Randall Coats, Catherine. *Subverting the System: d'Aubigné and Calvinism*. Vol. 16. Kirksville, M.I.: Sixteenth Century Essays and Studies, 1990.

Reiss, Timothy. *The Meaning of Literature*. Ithaca, N.Y.: Cornell University Press, 1992.

Richter, Mario. "A propos des 'Chrestiennes Méditations' de Théodore de Bèze. Essai de definition," in *La Méditation en prose à la Renaissance*, Cahiers V. L. Saulnier, no. 7. Paris: Presses de l'Ecole Normale Supérieure, 1990, pp. 59–75.

Soulié, Marguerite. *L'Inspiration biblique dans la poésie religieuse d'Agrippa d'Aubigné*. Paris: Klincksieck, 1977.

Sponde, Jean de. *Méditations avec un Essai de Poèmes chrétiens*. Edited by Alan Boase. Paris: José Corti, 1954.

Stegmann, André, ed. *Edits des guerres de religion*. Paris: Vrin, 1979.

Tirel, Pierre. "L'Education protestante jadis et naguère," in *La Réforme et l'éducation*. Sous la direction de Jean Boisset. Toulouse: Privet, 1974.

Toussain, Daniel. *L'Exercise de l'ame fidele, assavoir Prieres et Meditations pour se consacrer en toutes sortes d'afflictions*. MDLXXXII.

Trescases, Pierre. "La Naissance du discours linguistico-nationaliste ou le double mythe de la supériorité et de l'universalité du français." Unpublished manuscript.

La Vierge stigmatisée. Miracle nouvellement veu et appreuvé à Lisbonne en Portugal, à une tres devote religieuse de l'ordre de S. Dominique. Comme Jesuchrist nostre Seigneur, souventefois s'est apparu à elle, et luy a donné ces cinq playes et stigmates qu'il receut a la Croix. Discours tres proffitable à tous amateurs des graces de la vie Contemplative, dressé sur la relation des Peres dudit Ordre cy dernier nommez, envoyé de Lisbonne. Lyon: A la Bible d'Or, 1586.

Voloshinov, V. N. *Marxism and the Philosophy of Language*. Translated by Ladislav Matejka and I. R. Titunik. New York: Seminar Press, 1973.

Weber, Henri. *La Création poétique au XVIe siècle en France*. Paris: Nizet, 1955.

Studies in Reformed Theology and History

Studies in Reformed Theology and History, New Series

SUBSCRIPTIONS

The New Series will continue to be *gratis* to those who otherwise would not receive these studies.

For help in defraying the expense of printing and mailing, we are, however, suggesting the following scale: libraries, schools, centers, and institutes: $12 per monograph, individuals: $6 per monograph.

Note again: it is the aim of the Chair of the Editorial Council, the Editor and the Board of Trustees of Princeton Theological Seminary to continue to make this series available *gratis* to those who are unable to send the suggested subscription amount.

Checks should be made payable to: SRTH, Princeton Theological Seminary. The mailing address is: SRTH. Princeton Theological Seminary, P. O. Box 821, Princeton, NJ 08542-0803.

Back issues may be obtained for a mailing and handling charge according to the following rate:

1 issue	$2.00
2 issues	$4.00
3–9 copies	$5.00
10 or more	call the Theological Book Agency for information.

All back issue orders should be directed to: Theological Book Agency, P. O. Box 821, Princeton, NJ 08542-0803. Orders may also be placed by calling the Theological Book Agency at 609-497-7735. Make checks payable to TBA. U.S. funds only.

Name _____
         First   Middle   Last

Address _____
                 Institution, if applicable

_____
                 Department/Office

_____
                 Street

_____
         City   State   Country

_____
                 Postal Code

Please check one of the following:

☐ Institution or Library: $12.00 per volume
☐ Individual: $6.00 per volume
☐ Continue *gratis*